Moshe (Moshiko) I

Dancing Against the Flow

My warm thanks for:
Translation and publication of this work were
supported by Allen King with additional support of
Ruth (Browns) Gundelfinger.
English Editor: Larry Denenberg

Graphic Designer: Smadar Munis, Logoin
Translation from Hebrew: Chen Michaeli

ISBN 978-0-5788-3602-7

Printed in USA 2021

This book is dedicated to my children, grandchildren and great-grandchildren who inspired the melodies and dances that I composed and wrote.

My children: Uriah, Yiftach, Yochemed, Ben-Yah and Libi.

My grandchildren: Bosmat, Roi, Mor, Ariel, and Elay. Dor, Naor and Omer, Yiska and Reichan, Michael and Tamar.

My great-grandchildren: Yuvali, Ofir, Lior and Ori.

Special thanks to my wife Michal, who stands by me and helps me fulfill my dream. Without her, I doubt this book would have seen the light of day.

Table of Contents

Moshiko - Calling Card

Moshiko was born in 1932 in the Manshiya area near Kerem HaTeimanim.

Married + children, grandchildren and great-grandchildren, a choreographer, author, musician and choreographer integrating his creations with his compositions.

Moshiko made use of many styles such as: classical ballet, modern ballet, jazz, tap and folk dancing.

His dances excel at special style and draw influences from the ethnic origins found in Israel and the Mediterranean.

His dances are popular throughout Israel and worldwide.

Moshiko is a Yakir (Notable Person) of ACUM for his musical contribution to society.

He is also a Yakir of the Irgun HaMadrichim V'HaKoreographim in Israel.

Introduction

Dancing Against the Flow is the personal story that has accompanied my life, starting from childhood in south Tel-Aviv, through my professional journey in the world of Israeli folk dancing – in Israel and abroad – through to current times where I continue the course of my professional life in Israel and live happily with my family.

The book describes a long-lasting personal and professional struggle in Israeli society and the world of Israeli folk dancing, in an unceasing attempt to avoid being dragged after what existed and was popular, having faith that everything could be done differently.

With a clear mind I spent my entire life directing my efforts towards finding something else "ex nihilo", and "choosing my own way against the flow".

I was never afraid of facing challenges. I touched subjects and notions, in the areas of both musical choice and motion elements, which were unique and specific only to my way of working.

I did so throughout the years with the belief, which has stayed with me all this time, that the path I chose to walk was the only option for me, and the least disappointing, to this very day. There were difficult moments, where I almost lost hope and the will to continue working in folk dancing dwindled, and I even made the decision to quit, but events that occurred in my path encouraged me to change my decision. I thank God for giving me the strength to continue believing in the righteousness of my path.

Each of us has motives and reasons to write down the impressions and experiences which have accompanied us throughout our lives. These impressions and experiences are treasured in our minds and serve as waypoints. Sometimes they float to the surface and remind us of periods in our lives – some pleasant and some less so.

When I made the decision to write this book, I wondered whether to put down in writing the good parts that were apportioned to me and leave out the less good; whether to leave room for the disappointment I'd felt with people I'd respected and valued. After much deliberation I concluded that I couldn't ignore the difficulties that were an important factor in my professional development and my personal life. Likewise, I cannot deny the facts and the truth that have followed me along this path, and which in fact motivated me to begin writing my book.

I'm sure some readers will identify with me and some won't, and that is their prerogative.

The book is divided into three parts – Part A, The Family, discusses my childhood and adolescence; Part B, Dance Steps, tells of my professional life; Part C, Thoughts and Opinions, includes chapters I wrote wherein I expressed my personal opinions pertaining to the field of Israeli folk dancing.

I imagine you're very curious by now, so I'll simply wish you a pleasant reading experience.

Part A – The Family

Chapter 1

Childhood

I was born on the 3rd of July 1932, to my parents Shalom and Rachel, my sister Bracha and my paternal grandmother Badre (Deborah). Her presence at the birth of a son was a source of endless happiness for Grandmother – someone would carry the dynasty on…

My father, Shalom Yitzhak-Halevy, was born to a particularly well-off family from the Yitzhak-HaLevy dynasty. His family was known throughout Yemen due to the status and leadership of Rabbi Yechi Yitzhak-HaLevy – the head rabbi of Yemen's Jewry for 28 years. Rabbi Yichye and my grandfather Museh were cousins. At birth, I was given my grandfather's name – Moshe Yitzhak-Halevy.

My mother, father, grandmother, sister and me

My father, his mother's only son, was fatherless from birth, but my grandmother did everything she could to ensure he had a full and healthy childhood, with excellent education. And indeed, my father, who studied at the cheder in the Jewish ghetto in Sana'a, came to be considered a supreme authority in matters of religion as Jewish customs in Yemen. At 14 he passed all Kashrut tests in slaughtering animals and was certified as a butcher – a very esteemed and respected profession in the Jewish community.

But with his personal achievements came my father's appetite for adventure. At 11 he decided to run away from his home in Sana'a, and without his mother's knowledge he snuck into a convoy of camels carrying bags of legumes to Aden. The goods belonged to the famous Hibshush family who lived alongside the Yitzhak-Levys in the Jewish ghetto in Sana'a. The two families had a good relationship.

It was only when they'd gotten considerable distance from Sana'a that Yechiel Hibshush noticed my father but was forgiving and ensured he had everything he needed until they reached Aden, after an 11-day journey.

When my grandmother saw that her son had disappeared, she nearly lost her mind from worry, fearing for his life. It was only when people returned to Sana'a from Aden and told her of my father's whereabouts, and that he would return with the Hibshush convoy, that she calmed herself somewhat.

It would not be the last time my father fled to Aden. The British colonizers who ruled the city at the time introduced their culture, influencing the entire region. Modern life in Aden greatly appealed to my father.

He was 16 when he left Sana'a for the second and final time. He was gifted with a beautiful voice and a sense of humor, and so the Jewish residents of Aden would invite him to perform at events such as weddings, brit milahs, bar mitzvahs and other joyous occasions. His success in the artistic and entertainment fields, and the money he made there, tugged at his heartstrings.

During one of these events he saw my mother and admired her immediately. As the days passed it became clear she liked him as well.

Father began asking around about her, and once he had all the details he asked for her hand in marriage. Surprised and thrilled at the joyous news, Grandmother Badre began all the necessary preparations for a trip to Aden, for the henna and bridal ceremonies for her only son.

My family

My uncle Yechiel, my sister and me

Grandmother

Grandmother Badre was born in the city of Shibam in Yemen, eldest of three sisters – with Hamame and Benie. She was a stubborn woman who spoke her mind on all matters. She was the central and dominant figure in the family, and when her sisters married and each had their own family, my grandmother had a powerful influence on them as well. Of course, this was all done in accordance with the accepted traditions and customs of Yemen's Jewry, and out of respect to the eldest of the family in the event that the parents were not present or had passed on.

Another thing that characterized my grandmother was the large proportions of her body, both in height and width, unlike other Yemenite women who were usually small and thin.

Grandmother was my grandfather's second wife, and miraculously conceived at a relatively late age. With the birth of her only son Shalom her husband, my grandfather, passed away. Grandmother Badre kept a close watch over my father, protected him from harm and cared for him with endless devotion. The boy Shalom was the apple of her eye.

My father studied in a traditional cheder in Yemen. On one of those days, so my grandmother was informed, Father made an error while reading the Torah and was punished with a spanking from the mori (the traditional cheder teacher in Yemen). When Grandmother learned of this she reacted furiously and almost struck the mori. She warned him never to do so again – "that's why he has a mother!", she roared.

Mother

My mother Rachel was born in the city of Hasheish in Yemen, to Saadia and Bracha Hasheishi, the eldest of three sisters – Shoshana, and another sister whose name I do not know. Mother told me that one day, when she was a child watching over her little sister, she hoisted her up on her shoulders while playing, and the little girl fell backwards to the ground, and died.

When my grandmother learned of this, she pounced on my mother trying to strike her, but my grandfather shielded my mother with his body and told her: "Isn't it enough that we've lost a child, you want to kill another one?" There is no doubt this tragedy haunted my mother her whole life.

At a young age my mother lost her own mother, and though the burden of taking care of the entire family fell on her young shoulders, I never heard her complain about the difficult life that had been allotted to her. As a woman of faith, she accepted her fate with love and treated it as a divine decree.

Mother had to leave the village of Hasheish after her mother's death in order to find a source of income. After a difficult journey she reached Aden, where she was taken in by one of the wealthiest families in the city and worked in their home. The quality of her work, her reliability and decency earned her a safe position in her new family, which gave her a life without worry. The wealthy family considered my mother as a surrogate daughter, and ensured she wanted for nothing. She sent her savings to her father, to ease the daily difficulties of her family.

The wedding of my father and mother was also made possible thanks to that same wealthy family and the good neighbors who had introduced the young couple. Everyone did their best to ensure my parents' successful marriage, after which the two decided to make aliyah to Israel with my grandmother.

My mother

Coming to Israel

Mother, Father and Grandmother Badre left Aden on the deck of a boat that left the port of Djibouti towards Port Said in Egypt. From Egypt they took a train to Jerusalem, which at the time was a midway stop between Egypt and Damascus. When they reached Jerusalem, they stayed with the Shuker family – relatives, descendants of the Yitzhak-HaLevy family.

On Yom Kippur 1930, in the middle of prayer, my pregnant mother began to feel the pangs of labor that increased in power and frequency, heralding the birth of my sister Bracha. My grandmother, who was an accomplished midwife, delivered the baby with the help of the synagogue women. After the birth, and due to overcrowding at the Shuker residence, my grandmother decided to leave Jerusalem and we moved to Tel-Aviv.

We lived in a small apartment in the Manshiya area, on the border of Kerem HaTeimanim and the Hassan-Beck mosque and shared a yard with an Arab family. The area legally belonged to the jurisdiction of Jaffa, and was largely populated by Arab citizens, a fact that did not bother my family in the slightest. We lived in harmony with our neighbors.

In this yard, where I was born, our Arab neighbor's son was also born. When my mother went to the market or on errands, and I would cry, the Arab neighbor would nurse me. The same was true for my mother and the neighbor's son.

My Parents' Separation

But the ideal family was short-lived. From the moment we moved to Tel-Aviv my father stopped being the charming young man my mother had known in Aden. He was often absent from home, in the company of strange women, sometimes even bringing them home and hosting them without any consideration for my mother's feelings. Ultimately Father contracted an illness which he passed onto my mother, who had to undergo difficult and expensive medical treatments. She felt my father had violated her dignity and had gone too far.

I was nine months old when my mother decided to put an end to her relationship with my father and separate from him, but he rejected her and would evade any discussion on the subject with all sorts of excuses. She had to use all manners of ruses until she finally received the long-awaited divorce.

Grandmother Badre tried to dissuade my mother from her desire to divorce, promising she would do anything for her, support her and her children so long as she stayed in the house, but Mother was at the end of her rope and could not stay any longer. Once Grandmother understood that my mother's mind was made up in terms of separating from my father, she made only one request, to leave the children with her. "You're still young and without means. Leave the children here and you can start a new life." Mother had great respect for Grandmother Badre and trusted her. How could I raise them without money, and where would I leave them when I went to work, she wondered.

She was only sixteen – a very handsome woman with a long braid of hair that descended past her waist. With the news of her divorce, many men courted her in the hopes of marriage, but she rejected them all.

Father did not accept this situation, and even after the divorce he continued to bother her. He could not accept the fact that she was no longer his wife.

Despite her refusal of her suitors, Mother understood that it was not proper for a woman to be alone – a married woman, so she thought, would prevent harassment. She understood that if she married and rebuilt her life, my father would be forced to leave her alone.

Among the men who courted my mother was Saadia Darchi (from the village of Darach in Yemen) – a strong and muscled man who terrorized all of Kerem HaTeimanim and the Arabs of Jaffa. The Darchi families, led by Saadia Darchi, were always involved in fights and feuds with the Darda'im families1 of Kerem HaTeimanim. More than once the Darda'im ambushed Saadia Darchi and stunned him with their blows, but after a few days of recovery Saadia would have his revenge.

My mother found the answer to my father's harassment in Saadia Darchi and accepted his suit. Indeed, the moment he heard of the relationship between her and Saadia, my father left her alone. My mother married Saadia not out of love

---

1. The Darda'im: in 1914 Rabbi Yechi Kapach openly declared war on the book of the Zohar and the Kabbalists, and established the "Dor De'a" movement, causing a major dispute to erupt between them. The main opposition to Rabbi Kapach was Rabbi HaLevy and Rabbi Said Ozeri. They gave his movement and followers the mocking name "Darda'im". Rabbi Halevy's opposition claimed he was not popular with most of the people, and in 1920 (on a Saturday, while reading the Torah) a referendum was held between him and Rabbi Kapach. Its results revealed that Rabbi HaLevy was more popular with the majority of the public. Rabbi HaLevy had the upper hand and managed to unite an absolute majority of Yemenite Jewry and its rabbis around him, despite the politics that surrounded this dispute at the time.

but to ensure her own safety, yet he loved her most jealously. This was expressed more than once with bursts of rage and broken objects throughout the house.

My Stepfather Saadya Darhi

On days when he saw my mother was upset, Saadia knew what could pacify her, and without saying a word he would ride his bike to my grandmother's house to bring us for a quick visit with our mother. My grandmother didn't dare refuse Saadia, even she was intimidated by him.

And so, it was – Saadia would put my sister and I on his bike and we would ride with him walking beside us. I don't know what thrilled us more, riding the bike or meeting Mother. Despite my mother's agreement to leave her children with my grandmother, Grandmother was angry at her for leaving her son and marrying another and would banish her from her home without letting her see us. Twice, when Aunt Naomi (Naama) – daughter of my grandmother's sister Hamame – would walk with us on the beach, my mother would follow us and watch from afar. When she asked to approach, she was refused. My grandmother had instructed Naomi, with whom we spent much time growing up, not to allow our mother to approach.

Shivat Tzion

In 1936 the Arabs of Jaffa began persecuting the Jewish minority living among them. These riots caused great destruction, ruin and loss of life. Suddenly we were refugees in our own home. Our Arab neighbors begged my grandmother not to leave the neighborhood, and promised to protect us with their own bodies, but seeing the results of the riots Grandmother decided to join a large group of refugees in search of a haven.

We reached a building on Yehuda HaLevy Street in Tel-Aviv and entered a large lobby until the rage passed. My grandmother quickly understood that this was no solution. She left to wander the south of the city, seeking shelter for us.

She found an appropriate apartment in the Shivat Tzion neighborhood, with a price she could afford. Chanom, the Kurdish landlord, welcomed us, but it was no surprise the rent was relatively cheap; on the right side of the house was a dairy barn, with cows and the accompanying stench. But on the other hand, as if to balance out the bad smell, there was a bagel bakery with an unforgettable smell of fresh bread. Even the taste of bagels today isn't like the bagels of old.

The kindergarten of Aunt Chana (top left).
I am pictured in the top row, third from the left

After setting up in our new apartment, Grandmother had to earn income to support the cost of rent and food. Luckily Aunt Chana's kindergarten was located in the neighborhood and Grandmother could leave us there and go to work. My sister was only there for six months before graduating to first grade, whereas for me these were two pleasant years, eight hours a day of education, food and games.

To receive benefits from the social services department of the Tel-Aviv municipality, my grandmother claimed that my sister and I were orphans. No one questioned the truth of her words.

In our neighborhood everyone knew everything. Kurds lived there, and Iraqis, Yemenites and Ashkenazis. The owners of the dairy farm, for example, were Ashkenazis. One of the Iraqi families was raising two brothers, friends of mine. We would always play neighborhood games together. Years after we went our separate ways, I learned that one of the brothers became Chief of Staff of the Israeli Defense Force, none other than Moshe Levy (Moishe-and-a-half), may he rest in peace.

Giva'at Moshe Aleph

Dedicated to all the families of that precious neighborhood who were an inextricable part of my childhood landscape:

The fuzeilof Family – Bukharans

The Bechshein Family – Persians

The Shauli Family – Persians

The Azulai Family – Sephardic-Bukharans

The Sharafi Family – Persians

The Zar Family – Persians

The Eliazov Family – Kurdish

The Yesharim Family – Persians

The Bakhshi Family – Persians

The Nouri Family – Persians

The Anavi Family – Persians

The Nechama Family – Persians

The Shlush Family – Sephardic

After two years my grandmother's wanderlust awakened again, which this time led her a mere three hundred meters from Shivat Tzion, to the neighborhood of Giva'at Moshe Aleph, very near the house of her sister Hamame. Mostly Persian and Bukharan families lived there, along with three Yemenite families – Damari Hamame, the Yitzhak-HaLevy family and the Vashedi family.

At the center of the neighborhood was a large forum where we and an active group of youths gathered all the games that existed then – marbles (we called them bandores then), "dods", soccer, tag and more. There we lit the Lag Ba'Omer fires, the greatest of all the bonfires far and wide. The audience who came to witness our fiery demonstration was one of the largest in the area.

Every neighborhood event was assisted by all the neighborhood youths, with no exceptions. Our social integration showed itself both within and without the neighborhood. If we decided to go to a movie on Saturday night, the operation was planned down to the finest details: first – leaving the neighborhood, second – boarding the number 9 bus with us standing on the bus' rear bumper and holding onto the window. We had to scatter among several buses as there were twelve of us, third – meeting at Mugrabi Square with the "victim" of course being Mugrabi Cinema. After we made sure everyone had made it safely, we began collecting money to purchase just one ticket. We all wore the same "uniform" – a tank top and underwear. I was given the task of buying the ticket, walking in, and as soon as the lights went down I would go to the stairwell and open the doors. To deceive the ushers our friends would split into groups, each entering from a different door. We usually succeeded. Once we were in the theater we would scatter among the rows. Merciful viewers would help us hide between their legs and let us enjoy the movie. These operations were repeated again and again during our adolescence, and throughout the week we would enjoy talking about the experience.

On weeknights we would light a small bonfire at the center of the neighborhood. We would throw potatoes and onions into the fire, eat them and enjoy them, and when our stomachs and hearts were full we would break out into mighty song. Either the neighborhood residents would leave their houses to join our singing, or… it was usually my grandmother who would put an end to the joy by loudly calling out "Moshe, Moshe…" and said that if I didn't come home at once I would have to sleep in the street.

I was the life of the party and one of the leaders of the group. The moment I had to leave, the festivities would be over, and the group would scatter to their homes.

In the early morning hours, Grandmother would wake my sister or me, give us a milk jug and send us to purchase goat milk from the Arab shepherds who would come to the neighborhood with their herds. The neighborhood residents would stand in line to purchase the fresh milk, drawn straight from the udder. We had a very good relationship with the Arabs who lived adjacent to our neighborhood. They had orchards of oranges, grapefruit, clementines and lemons, and they provided us with abundance.

As the Passover holiday approached groups of Arabs would arrive who specialized in making houseware Kosher, and the housewives would gather with their pots and wait to cleanse them for Passover. The holiday atmosphere was felt throughout the neighborhood. The brave relationships with the Arabs added a special pastoral and folkloric beauty to our lives in this country. It is a beauty I'm sorry to say no longer exists.

Yesod Ha'Maaleh Elementary School

Yesod Ha'Maaleh Elementary School was located near the old central station. Even in my junior grades I was the naughty student who raised hell for teachers, especially our homeroom teacher **Mordechai Kletzky**. For example, during tests I would fill my pants pockets with sunflower seeds, and since I was among the first to finish the test, I would ask Kletzky to excuse me from class. Of course, he absolutely refused. And then… I would start cracking open the seeds I'd brought. The noise disrupted the class. When I noticed Kletzky's anger, and that he was about to catch and punish me, I would flee the class.

The classroom's window on the second floor faced the street, and the sewage pipe that ran along the building's wall allowed me to climb up and peek through the window. My prank would distract the teachers and drive the teacher mad, and then, as a ruse of his own, Kletzky would open the window and ask me to step into class. I innocently thought this was the end of the affair, but of course I was wrong. The moment I entered class Mr. Kletzky grabbed me and dragged me to another building's second floor, to the principal's office, with me hanging from his body unable to free myself.

The school principal would punish students by striking their fingertips with a large ruler. But fortunately for me, when I was brought to his room, he was on his way out to a previous commitment. He locked me in his room and prepared to punish me when he returned. To his disappointment and my joy, I managed to escape through the window, again using the sewage pipe…

I excelled at sports and music. Hoffman, the music teacher, was interested in Yemenite songs and melodies, and invited me to his home on Saturdays. I made my way to his home on foot, down Salame Street in south Tel-Aviv, to the corner of King Solomon and Gordon at the north part of town. I was pleased that I could contribute some of the knowledge I'd been imprinted with in my father's house. Today I would define Mr. Hoffman as more of a musicological researcher than a music teacher.

Aliyah A

At the end of fourth grade, due to behavioral problems, it was decided that I would be transferred to Aliyah A, a school where difficult students were sent from several schools in Tel-Aviv. The school's teachers were chosen especially for their toughness, to handle students like us.

One of my habits at school was lifting chairs and tables using my teeth, something no other student dared to do. I'd always been competitive, liking to do things that made me feel like there was no one out there who was as brave as me. I remember one incident when a truck unpacked sand, and a small dune formed at the front of the school. I climbed to the third floor of the school building and jumped into the dune. I was always looking for challenges that would send adrenaline racing through my body. I never saw any danger flash before my eyes that I could resist.

One time I walked into a raging ocean, and felt I was having trouble returning to the shore. The waves swept me deeper into the sea. I drifted further and further, despite my efforts to fight the waves, but I didn't call for help. For me it was a matter of honor.

I felt there was no point in fighting the waves. I believed I would survive, I was optimistic. I tried to float on the water and conserve my strength, and slowly felt the waves I'd been struggling against previously were pushing me back onto the shore. When my feet finally touched sand, I lay down and fell asleep. When I awoke, I thought about what had happened. I hadn't feared death. I knew someone above was putting me to the test and wanted to see how I would handle difficult situations.

Between Grandmother's House and Mother's

Life at my grandmother's house became more and more difficult. We had little in common. I felt bound to her and the anger between us grew louder and more intolerable. More than once I found myself having to leave the house and stay with my friends Benyamin and Mordechai Shimoni, may they rest in peace. They lived in HaTikva neighborhood, very close to my mother's house. My friends' families had undergone some tragedies – their father had died young when the two were toddlers; their elder brother was involved in a murder and spent many years in prison. When he was released, he left the country for fear of a blood vendetta; Mordechai Shimoni was killed in a parachuting accident in the army; his brother Benyamin, who loved him with every fiber of his being, couldn't endure the pain and died as well; and finally, the poor mother's heart gave out and she passed on as well. These tragic events haunted me all my days – and continue to do so today. I felt, and still feel, the despair of that long-suffering family.

My visits with my mother weren't frequent, but always spontaneous. As soon as I felt some inner urge to be with her, I would go. Sometimes she would not be home, and I would have to retrace my steps, but when I was lucky enough to meet her she would set aside anything else and be with me completely. She was eager to hear everything I was going through, and sometimes would tell me a bit about herself as well. With every visit she would give me an allowance, which I'd never received from my father or grandmother.

I don't blame my grandmother, she worked hard to support the household and care for us. She never had any money to spare, on the contrary – she always had to borrow money to keep us alive. She worked from early morning to late at night with her sister Hamame, laundering and hand-ironing bed sheets at one of the Tel-Aviv hotels.

During one especially rainy winter day, while I was still living at my grandmother's, I decided to visit my mother. On the way I passed the old Ayalon Bridge on HaHagana street. On the bridge, which was flooded with rainwater, I saw a group of children tormenting a small dog, trying to drown him while he was bound with an improvised leash around his neck.

The children's prank infuriated me. I ran towards them, and during the fight I managed to pull the dog away from them. He was shaking not just because of the cold but out of fear as well. I tried to calm him down. I turned around and returned to my grandmother's house to take care of him, and make sure he had a warm corner to rest.

The house's backyard had a wooden shed. I fed the dog and gave him water. He was too aggressive, not understanding there were people who wanted what was best for him. I pitied him and wanted very much to adopt him, but I knew I could never do so without my grandmother's consent. I brought him to the shed, locked the door to keep him from running away, and retraced my steps again, on my way to my mother.

By the time I returned from my mother, my grandmother had not yet returned from work. I waited nervously and anxiously for her, and when she arrived, I told her about the dog. She adamantly objected. I asked her to consider letting the dog stay with us for just a few days, until he recovered from the trauma he'd endured, but she refused this request as well.

I was angry. I warned her that if she drove the dog away, I would do something she would regret, but she didn't take my threats seriously. The next morning, when I was a mere thirty meters away from the house, I saw the dog fleeing for his life from the shed. I was furious and ran home to make good on my threat.

My grandmother had a white closet with a big mirror, the only mirror in the house. I kicked it twice, shattering it to pieces, and with the sound of Grandmother's curses and threats in my ear I ran to my mother's house, where she welcomed me happily.

Days of Forgiveness

Several weeks after the dog incident, my grandmother began sending messages to me that she wanted me to return home. It was the month of Tishrei, and the Ten Days of Tshuva. I knew this was the time to ask forgiveness and make peace. My father would do the same every Rosh HaShana, after being absent from home almost every day of the year. He would come to his mother's house, lie on the floor and kiss her feet. Then he would rise up and kiss her hands and face. I could see how much my grandmother enjoyed this ritual, which reminded her of the customs of Yemen. I couldn't help snickering, knowing the problems my father had caused my grandmother, my sister and I throughout the year (more on that in a later chapter). I came to my grandmother as well, but this ritual was short. I kissed her hands and asked for her forgiveness. I felt I'd done my duty; at eleven I no longer believed that asking forgiveness would prevent the next incident.

Cantillation Notes

The year was 1943. I returned to school at Aliyah A – repeating fourth grade – in a superhuman attempt to hold on. I had a good friend in class named Dudu Chever. If someone in class tried to pick on my good friend I could skip over desks in the middle of class, reach the bully and "settle the score".

Our Cantillation Notes teacher was **Nissan Cohen-Melamed**, a strict and tough teacher who ran his classes with an iron hand. Fourth graders were terrified of him, and if he had to strike a student who was acting out, he would do so without hesitation. At the same time Cohen-Melamed had a pleasant voice, and a wonderful talent for trilling out cantillation notes.

I loved his classes and excelled at them, while in other classes I'd go wild. When Mr. Melamed heard the complaints of other teachers towards me, he would ask to have a private conversation with me and try to set me straight, but it never lasted – I would go back to my old ways very quickly.

I lasted less than six months at Aliya A before being expelled. My grandmother tried to convince the school principal to take me back, to no avail. I started thinking about my future. I concluded that I had to leave town and find a place where I could prepare myself for a better future.

My grandmother approached the Tel-Aviv Municipality's social services department, asking for me to be accepted to some youth institution. It turned out there were other boys in the Tel-Aviv area with an urgent need to find an institution that was appropriate for them. We were told that by the end of 1943 the proper solution would be found for us. In the meantime, I continued to hang out with the children of Giva'at Moshe Aleph. Our activities bordered on criminality more than once. When we were hungry, we would go to Aliya Market on Aliya Street, where there were food stands outside the store. While running one of us would snatch a loaf of bread, another cheese, the third a bottled drink, and after our mission was carried out, we would enter one of the shelters in the area and satiate our hunger. Despite being minors, we were afraid of getting caught and finding ourselves in prison. But we were ruled by hunger and the urge for adventure.

We repeated these acts dozens of time, but fortunately and much to our pleasure we were never caught. After a few weeks the social services department of Tel-Aviv Municipalities sent us a reply. The institution they'd found for me was Har-Tov, near Beit-Shemesh.

I was thrilled and couldn't wait to head out to the institution. I prepared my neighborhood friends in advance. I had no doubts at all – I'd already started planning my new life.

My grandmother, my sister and her children Yael and Moti

Chapter 2

The Pedagogic Poem of Tzvi Giva'ati and the Har-Tuv Children

The date of departure to the "Har-Tuv" Youth Institute arrived. We met in June 1944 at the southern train station, by the road to Petach Tikva (today Menachem Begin Road). From afar only lone boys were visible, but as the minutes passed more and more arrived. We stood at the station – sixty to seventy excited boys. A young and handsome man joined us. "My name is Zvi Berg," he introduced himself, "and I'm the instructor in charge of you."

The train to Jerusalem arrived and we were swallowed into one of the cars. At Ramleh Station we disembarked and were picked up by a bus to Jerusalem. We got off at the Sha'ar HaGai station and started walking towards the Har-Tuv settlement – seven kilometers away, at the end of which we had to climb up the mountain. On the way we passed Zar'aa and Eshteol Kibbutz. For me it was the first excruciating journey in my life, but I didn't complain, no one did – we all met the task heroically.

We reached a small settlement built adjacent to an Arab village. The settlement was populated by several families of farmers hailing from Bulgaria. I looked around. The place looked like a real dream – surrounded by green forest and a spectacular view. We went to tour the Institute's facilities. We visited our two-story dormitory, the office building for the administration and instructors, the large cafeteria, the welding classroom, the carpentry workshop, the school classroom and the petting zoo.

We were split into three groups – mature, average and young – and accordingly into the rooms as well, four or five per room. I was in the eldest group.

After a brief conversation about the area, the lesson plan and the work, and after dinner, we scattered to our rooms, but I was sleepless. The excitement overcame my exhaustion and my mind was full of thoughts – I was starting a new life here, building my future, and from now on I would have a place to call my own. I wouldn't have to worry about food, from this day on the teachers and instructors were my parents, I had to do my best as much as I could for my good future.

My Purim picture with Avraham Karako

Half a Day of Work, Half a Day of School

I must have finally dozed off, because when I awoke the sun was already shining. After breakfast we went to work. The plan was to spend half a day working and half a day studying in the afternoon. Since I was learning the profession of carpentry on behalf of the Tel-Aviv Municipality's social services division, which employed children after school hours, I decided to learn welding. I have no doubt that carpentry and welding both trained me for a future of entrepreneurship and implementing ideas and challenges that accompanied me for the rest of my life.

When the workday was over we would have lunch and rest for a while. How good it was to go back to class after a long period of being absent, with no books, notebooks or pencils. At Har-Tuv we received everything for free – all you had to do was reach out and take the opportunity being given to you…

We met our teacher **Barkai** and the team of professional instructors led by Zvi Berg (soon to be Giva'ati) who we had already met at the train station. Among the children was a group of twenty-two boys, mostly Yemenites, called "the jungle group". These were boys who had taken over a place formerly called the Maxim Club, which had been frequently visited by soldiers of the British army, on Yarkon Street in Tel-Aviv (in front of what is currently the American embassy). These were troubled boys who had left their homes, and Zvi Berg, who had been a scout leader, gathered them under his wing. In preparation for the Institute Zvi found an abandoned structure in Ramat HaSharon, and along with the boys he tore out the weeds and cleansed the area in preparation for what was to come.

Forty other boys were added to the jungle group, including me. Zvi had captured all our hearts with his fatherly approach and pleasant words. We loved him and acknowledged his authority. He was there for us twenty-four hours a day, and at night he would ensure we were all in our beds, healthy and whole. We could talk to Zvi about anything, at any time, ask questions, make requests – and he always responded with kindness. He gave us all a sense of safety, he educated us and showed us the light at the end of the tunnel.

The welding workshop was managed by **Netanel**, a quiet professional whose work with his students was exceptional. I can say of myself that my two years in the workshop contributed greatly and helped me several times in my life.

After Netanel we were taught welding by our instructor **Federbush**. Federbush would marry **Naomi Levy** of the **Levy Family**, who along with the **Bachar Family** were among the founders of the settlement. Naomi worked at the Institute and was a great boon to us.

The professional instructor **Terry** was in charge of the carpentry workshop. He was a Yemenite man who, along with having great knowledge of carpentry, was also a wonderful flute player. Terry was a source of inspiration to me, for fulfilling the dream that someday I might play as he did.

And indeed, on my thirteenth birthday I asked my sister Bracha to buy me a flute. When I received it, none could be happier. I would flee into the nearby forest with sandwiches, sit there for hours and play. For an entire month I taught myself to play about forty songs. Playing the flute transformed me from an introverted, insecure child to a popular guest at any social event.

Mr. Barkai was in charge of the classroom. He was a pleasant and serious man, with a positive attitude towards every single student. One of the students who excelled in our class was **Moshe Cohen**. I remember this, because Mr. Barkai tasked us with memorizing a certain literary passage, but no one except Moshe Cohen succeeded. When his turn came, he stood up and fluently, confidently began reciting the passage. The teacher, who was already familiar with his abilities, asked him to stop, but Moshe kept going. When Mr. Barkai saw that Moshe would not stop, he took a glass of water that was lying on his table and splashed it in Moshe's face, but Moshe kept reciting – all the way to the end… I will remember that incident for the rest of my life. Of course, it was entertaining and in good spirits.

The person in charge of our "wardrobe" – laundry and ironing – was **Esther Bachar**, a Har-Tuv daughter who would go on to marry Zvi Berg. Esther was like a caring mother to us. It is no wonder that even after so many years, most of the Institute children remember the contribution and influence of Zvi and Esther.

Another person I want to mention was connected to the security of the Har-Tuv settlement. This was **Aharon Levy**, who rarely separated from the horse he rode. Aharon was also responsible for bringing water to the settlement and solved and repaired any other maintenance problem.

Last but not least, I remember the stout man who was in charge of kitchen supplies – **Mr. Koffman**. His job was to ensure the quality of the food for the Institute's children. Unfortunately, both the quality and quantity were low, which stirred our anger. We arranged a student rebellion at the Institute, during which we broke into the food warehouse and caused a great amount of destruction. Only after Zvi Berg's intervention, and after we were promised that the situation would improve, did we relent. And indeed, over time we saw a significant improvement.

The Kfar Gilladi Work Camp

Zvi Berg was also in charge of cultural activities at the Institute. Every Friday evening, we would have Sabbath receptions in which I would participate, either by reading or singing or playing the flute. Our Sabbath receptions became a point of interest for the residents of Har-Tuv, who would cluster around the windows of our cafeteria and listen to the program. We felt great pride and accomplishment at our ability to do positive things not just for ourselves but for society as well.

We put on shows during special events and holidays, we went on trips, but the crown jewel was the "work camp" at Kfar Gilladi in the Galilee. It wasn't a simple arrangement to make. Zvi had to convince the kibbutz secretary that there was no need to fear accepting former street children for a week of work. He promised we would behave ourselves, and so we did.

Zvi Giva'ati, Naomi Levy and the Har-Tuv Children. Kfar Gilladi Work Camp

The Kibbutz prepared a tent camp for us on a broad platform surrounded by little stones, painted white. At the center of the camp was a pole to wave the national flag. The flag was raised early in the morning, before heading out to work, and lowered in the evening. Despite the less-than-ideal conditions, I remember that week of work as a foundational, unforgettable time.

We picked tomatoes and apples. I remember that at the end of our work in the tomato patch there were pesticides on our hands that wouldn't come off. We tried cleaning our hands with water and soap, we tried stronger materials, but nothing helped – a sticky, troublesome layer remained on our hands. A kibbutz member solved the problem: only tomato juice would remove the layer of pesticides from our hands, he said, and wonder of wonders – within seconds the feeling and natural color had returned to our hands.

Ultimately the kibbutz was satisfied with our help and expressed their thanks with several boxes of apples. Zvi was proud of us, and we were full of adrenaline and happiness as we returned to our clean and beloved corner of Har-Tuv.

What We Did and Where We Went

Most of the Institute graduates who pursued independent lives integrated into society and did their part – whether in culture, art, sports or security – all thanks to the education we received and the positive influence Zvi Berg (Giva'ati) had on us. We walked in Zvi's light and thanks to him we managed to shake ourselves free of the past and build a new, better world for us and our children.

I remember some of my friends, initiates of Har-Tuv, and want to share with you their achievements and contributions to society. I'm sure there are many more of our friends, in Israel and around the world, who did their best, and perhaps continue to do so.

Shlomo Drori (Chidefi) was among the first to leave Har-Tuv, joining Geva kibbutz. After a year and a half in the kibbutz he enlisted in the army and served in the Armor division, where he happened to meet Zvi (Berg-Giva'ati) at Zrifin Base. The meeting created joint work instructing wayward children in Jerusalem. Zvi found several buildings in the German colony of Katamon, and that was where they operated.

For twenty-two years Shlomo Drori worked in the field, six of which he spent as an educational coordinator, during which he studied Adolescent Education at the Hebrew University on Mount Scopus and was certified in Education. For a certain period, he worked at the Messila Institute in Jerusalem, and then at locating gangs of wayward children and treating them on behalf of the Jerusalem Municipality. After fifteen years he retired.

Avner Yefet was in that first group to leave Har-Tuv. Avner was always a good-natured person and never took life too seriously. During the War of Independence he joined the ranks of Etzel and was among the warriors who conquered Jaffa. In the battle for Jaffa he was injured and lost one of his legs. But even on crutches Mr. Avner kept his spirits up. Several years after his injury, he contracted a degenerative disease he could not overcome.

Avraham David kept in touch with the Institute even after he left. During the War of Independence, when the Institute children had to be relocated to Jerusalem and from Jerusalem to Tel-Aviv, Avraham would visit every weekend and assist the team of instructors.

During his dance classes at Mia Arbatova's studio, Avraham discovered **Moshe Gamliel** among the Har-Tuv initiates, a boy with a rare talent for dance, catching and execution. Avraham would teach Gamliel dance and tap moves.

Avraham David's military service was spent in the military band with me. When I was discharged the band was transferred to Northern Command and Avraham was among the founders of the Northern Command Band.

After a year of studies funded by the Army, Avraham heard that the director Menachem Golan was looking for candidates for his play El Dorado. He approached him, passed the audition and was accepted. Afterwards he took part in other performances. Having caught the theater bug Avraham decided to teach at the London School of High Arts, and when he returned to Israel he was invited to HaBima to direct two plays: "Little Killers" and "His Reputation Precedes Him" by Efraim Kishon. He later wrote plays and appeared in Israeli settlements with a group of actors on behalf of "Art for the Nation".

Pinchas Bar-David (Mizrahi) left upon graduating from the Institute for training at Beit HaShita kibbutz. He served in Battalion 82 of the Armor division as a tank operator and commander. During Operation Kadesh he substituted for his injured commander, and for this he received an officer's rank without the requisite course. After the Six Day War he underwent a tank battalion commander course and was appointed tank battalion commander and battalion commander of the Siyur brigade.

After the Yom Kippur War he was appointed Deputy Battalion Commander, received the rank of lieutenant colonel and was appointed division commander of reserve forces. At the same time he managed projects at the Tel-Aviv Municipality's water plant and emergency services division. In light of his considerable experience he was appointed Vice Administrative Manager of the Municipality's Engineering and Division Administration. After 44 years he retired, and spent thirteen years as the Retiree Chairman of Tel-Aviv Municipality.

Avraham Michaeli was recruited to Southern Command in 1949 and served at Eilat Fortress. After he was discharged, he was accepted as a tax clerk at Tel-Aviv Municipality and served as an urban inspector for thirty years.

Pinchas Abhar moved to Beit Alpha kibbutz where he stayed for four years. He was recruited into Golani and served for some time in the Northern Command band, under the command of Avraham David. When he completed his service, he became a driver for Egged, and then a wayward youth instructor at a branch of HaNo'ar HaOved, and as a branch coordinator in Haifa. Pinchas dedicated 25 years to youth, during which he studied economics, education and employment laws at Haifa University.

Mordechai Tuberi was part of the younger class of Har-Tuv children. After completing his studies, he joined the Dgania Bet group and Ramat-David kibbutz. He spent his military service as a sapper in the Giva'ati division.

When he was discharged, he returned to the city and became a sub-contractor for water lines in the Heirut area of Jerusalem. He was later hired at the Avik pharmaceutical company and served in maintenance for twenty-five years.

After Avik was purchased by the Teva pharmaceutical corporation, Mordechai continued working there for another fifteen years.

Yosifun Shachar (Mizrachi) served in the Israeli Air Force. After completing his service, he joined the Tel-Aviv HaPoel orchestra as a clarinet player, conducted by **Yitzhak Graziani**, and later joined the Tel-Aviv City Hall Choir with which he performed for nearly three years.

As I write these lines, I have learned of Yosifun's untimely passing due to pneumonia and the collapse of his immune system.

I had a special connection with him. For seven years Yosifun and his wife would spend every Wednesday in my folklore dance classes. He would solve crosswords while his wife danced and would enjoy the variety of melodies heard at the class. Even when his wife stopped coming, he kept showing up. May his memory be a blessing.

Rachamim Adani was one of the most wonderful recorder players at the Har-Tuv Institute. He also learned to play the clarinet, like Yosifun, and also joined the Tel-Aviv HaPoel orchestra conducted by Yitzhak Graziani. Rachamim lived in London for several years and had British citizenship. Today he lives in Israel.

Moshe Cohen was in my opinion the best graduate of Har-Tuv. Today he and his children manage a Mizrachi restaurant.

There is not enough time or space to fully describe the public activities of **David Zvi**. As a youth he was hired by the Dan company and became a committee member. At the municipal elections to Tel-Aviv City Hall Zvi was elected to the city council as a representative of the Herut movement. Zvi served in several symbolic functions at the Herut movement until he retired. Today Zvi manages the Likud branch near Tel-Aviv City Hall.

After two years at Har-Tuv I left the institute and moved to the kibbutz (more on that in the next chapter). Before the War of Independence broke out, my friends who remained at the Institute had to leave Har-Tuv and move to Jerusalem until the furor passed. Then they wandered to Tel-Aviv, to Ramat Amidar. In our free time we would still meet – Avraham David and I – as we were soulmates, but in time our paths separated as well.

Our Man at the Har-Tuv Institute

Dedicated to the Instructor and Educator Zvi Giva'ati (Berg) RIP – 2015

I walked the long way
to reach the very best
From you I learned what mattered
You taught me never to give up

To believe there was a ray of light
That good was out there somewhere
All you had to do was try
to get there

And I did get there, and I did find it
And I reached the very peak of glory
Because of what I learned from you
Through faith and prayer

Your name is engraved on the walls of my heart
Carried on my lips
Remembered in the depths of my soul
And I will remember you forever

May your soul be bound up in the bonds of life
and rest in Eden.
From your student, Moshe Yitzhak-HaLevy – Moshiko

Ziva Giva'ati and his wife, Esther

Zvi Giva'ati and his grandaughter

Zvi Giva'ati and Tel-Aviv Mayor Ron Huldai in a special ceremony for Zvi Giva'ati's lifetime achievement, at City Hall

With Ron Huldai, mayor of Tel Aviv

The Har-Tuv graduates

The Har-Tuv children with Ron Huldai, Mayor of Tel-Aviv, and Zvi Giva'ati

Chapter 3

Kibbutz Days

After two years at Har-Tuv, the Institute's administration contacted me and informed me that as I was among their top students, I could conclude my journey at the Institute and set out for an independent life. Two options were presented to me – I could return home, meaning to my grandmother's house in Tel-Aviv, or set out for a training program at a kibbutz. The latter idea appealed to me far more. I was only fifteen and feared I would be unable to cope with city life and be tempted to fall back into everything that had caused me to leave. I decided to go to the kibbutz. The Institute administration approached several kibbutzim to find the right place for me. We waited for an answer.

The answer came some weeks later. The Givot Zayid kibbutz in Emek Izrael approved my acceptance. A consolidated group that had previously been trained at Alumot kibbutz by Lake Kineret was already operating there. I joined the group.

Givot Zayid was a relatively young kibbutz that based its activities on the legacy of Alexander Zayid, blessed be his memory – among the outstanding individuals in the second wave of immigration, and one of the organizers of the guarding organizations Bar Giyora, HaShomer, HaKibbutz and Agudat HaShomrim.

After the murder of Alexander Zayid in 1938, his wife Zippora – an exemplary woman – and her children Yiftach, Giyora, Yochanan and Kochava remained. The children were greatly admired: Yiftach was a Mediterranean light-heavyweight boxing champion, and the others were excellent athletes as well. In fact, the entire Zayid family was involved with sports.

Kibbutz life appealed to me and I was sure I'd found my place. I worked in crop cultivation, orchards and the bakery.

The work in the crops and orchards was in areas outside the kibbutz, and rides to the workplace were not always possible, especially when returning, when I was already hungry and exhausted. I often found myself walking back to the kibbutz, a difficult trek to the looming mountain of Emek Izrael. I was very happy to reach my room and my bed.

A Tractor Story

One day as I was finishing my work with the crops, and making my way back up to the kibbutz, a tractor loaded with members of the training group pulled up behind me. It was obvious there was no room for me, and that the tractor wouldn't stop. I decided to block it with my body. I stood in the middle of the road and wouldn't let it pass. Everyone sitting there yelled that there was no room for me, but I stood my ground. Then I instructed one of the people sitting there to get off. He wouldn't. I pulled him off. None of the others dared protest my behavior.

After pulling the guy off the tractor we had an exchange of words that infuriated and offended me. I slapped him. Silence fell upon us all. None of the trainees dared defy me in any way.

I was impulsive and inconsiderate. My vocabulary was poor, and I solved all my problems through brute force. I had assimilated these habits I'd brought with me from the streets I'd wandered through as a child.

When I mounted the tractor to take my place, the guy shouted that I didn't know how to talk and that not everything could be achieved through force. I instructed the driver to get moving. The guy I'd pulled down walked home.

While I made it to the kibbutz, the trainee's words haunted me. To this day the misdeed troubles my conscience. I skipped dinner and went to bed, feeling ashamed and disgraced.

With the dawn I awoke to a new day with a fateful decision – from that day on I would never raise a hand against anyone, I would speak less and listen more, and enrich myself with a vocabulary that would allow me to express myself and my way of thinking. It was a decision that took years to realize, and this is an opportunity to ask forgiveness from that trainee whose name, **Avraham Kira**, I never forgot. If I could talk to him today, I would tell him he was the one who changed my life and made me a different person, for which I am grateful to him each and every day.

I was the group's living spirit and their entertainer. In the evenings we would gather at the club for various cultural activities, usually including folk dancing. Along with our training instructor there was a pianist, and when he heard me playing the flute, he tried to teach me classical pieces – him on the piano and me on the flute. I removed all the benches from the hall and encouraged the whole gang to start dancing. First, we danced the Hora for a very long time, and only then did we move on to the Krakoviak, the Cherkessia and the polka. Those were unforgettable evenings.

My tendency to entertain was probably something I'd inherited from my father. I would perform for my friends in the group, whether by playing the flute, telling amusing stories or making funny impersonations. My friends predicted that I'd make it to Hollywood someday. They weren't that far off – over the years I made some of my dreams come true, and during one trip with the Inbal dance troupe we did indeed make it to Hollywood…

After two years in the Kibbutz my sister notified me that she was about to get married and would move away; she asked me to return home to Tel-Aviv in order to assist my grandmother financially. The kibbutz granted me a year's leave, at the end of which I would be able to return. I hoped I would be able to do so.

Chapter 4

⊚⊚⊚⊚⊚⊚⊚⊙ ⊙⊙⊙⊚⊚⊚⊚

My Mother, My Parent – Stories from Mother's House

During my brief vacations in my Har-Tuv and Givot Zayid days, I would visit my mother who lived in HaTikva neighborhood. We didn't have phones to coordinate, and so I would drop by unannounced. I was greatly disappointed when I didn't find her at home, but when I arrived and she was there, I was welcomed with excitement and warmth. There is no substitute for maternal warmth – my mother's love was essential to me, something I'd lacked since I was nine months old.

My mother was a humble and constricted person, who had great difficulty expressing her feelings. And yet, I felt her love well through her hugs and kisses. I loved the delicious food she made, and when nothing was available during a visit, my mother would improvise a fish stew with spicy sauce and warm pitas fresh from the oven, and all sorts of other meals, so she could enjoy watching me eat.

After the meal, Mother would hand me a prayer book to recite the Birkat HaMazon prayer; as a religious woman she believed one must thank the Lord not just for food, but for all things we enjoy.

Afterwards we would sit and talk. She would share her experiences with me and tell stories that were sometimes hair-raising. More than once I asked myself how she had survived everything she had endured in life.

For the Sake of Dignity

During her marriage to my stepfather, Saadia Darhi, my mother was not blessed with children. My stepfather Saadia blamed my mother for this, even though she had delivered two children during her first marriage. When he was told the problem might lie with him he refused to accept this and sent my mother for medical testing.

To maintain the peace at home and for the sake of his dignity my mother did as he demanded. When the tests were concluded the doctor told her: "Madame, you could get pregnant with a kiss." But even then, my stepfather refused to accept the verdict and went to get tested. To solve the problem in a way that would not harm his pride, my mother suggested matching him with a second wife, who could perhaps provide him with a child. When a woman was found for him, Mother escorted the couple to the head rabbinical office, and before the eyes of the astonished rabbis she gave her consent to her husband's marriage. She even cleared one of the rooms in the house for the "young couple".

After a year, during which my mother did everything she could to aid the couple, the marriage ran aground. The second wife did not conceive. My stepfather asked my mother to see to his divorce. My mother did so by offering financial compensation, and the other woman went her way.

Two Weeks That Became Eighteen Years

In the War of Independence there were Arabs from the village of Shalem, near the HaTikva neighborhood, who would fire at the houses in the neighborhood. Some bullets even struck the blinds in the room my sister shared with her husband after they were married and lived for a time with my mother and stepfather. My sister was afraid to continue living there and decided to move to a safer place.

When her room was free my mother met a family in the street who were fleeing Shalem village, and sought an apartment for only two weeks. My mother, who always aided the less fortunate, agreed to host the family. But after two weeks, when it was time for them to vacate the room, they refused. They refused after a month, and then for eighteen years… a nightmare accompanied by violent incidents and court cases.

During one incident, matters escalated to the point where the tenant struck my mother in the head, causing bleeding in her head and ear. Mother filed a lawsuit against him, but the trial was conducted sloppily, and nothing resulted from it. It turned out that the tenant had a friend who was a sergeant in the police. When he heard what his friend had done, and of the physical damage done to my mother, he suggested that the tenant join the police, promising that when he appeared in court in police uniform he would be acquitted. And so it was. The judge was impressed by the tenant's opinion and dismissed my mother's claims. After the trial the tenants took matters a step further and told my mother that not only would they not leave the house, they would force her to leave instead.

As a religious woman, my mother had difficulty processing this cruel reality. She had always believed that "emissaries of good deeds are not harmed" (Pesachim 8), but in this case she had no idea where to find salvation. She continued to pray and believe that God would not let her down and that salvation would arrive. And indeed, after seventeen years the policeman tenant was caught stealing. He was ejected from the police and stripped of all privileges. A short while later the tenant fell ill and passed away. After the father died, my mother's tenants left the house, but not before receiving financial compensation from her.

The tenant's friend and his wife would often get involved in the quarrel and spared no curse directed at my mother. When the wife was pregnant my mother said: "I pray no son is born to you." When she heard this, the wife screamed at my mother: "Who are you, God?!" To this my mother replied: "If there is a God, he will answer my prayer."

And indeed, in each of that woman's seven pregnancies only daughters were born. The couple began to fight amongst themselves because the husband wanted an heir to carry on the family name, and they even considered divorce. During her eighth pregnancy, which was meant to be the last attempt, the woman saw my mother by the synagogue on Yom Kippur. With tears in her eyes she approached my mother, threw herself on the ground trying to kiss my mother's feet, apologized for all the misdeeds she and her husband had caused, and asked my mother to bless her pregnancy. My mother couldn't resist her pleas. She placed both hands on the woman's belly and said: "I pray that with this Yom Kippur a son is born to you," and wonder of wonders – after seven daughters, a male child was born to the family.

At the lowest point in her relationship with the tenants living in my mother's house and refusing to leave, something happened. A coin was stuck in the throat of their young child. He turned blue and began to choke. My mother, hearing the neighbor's cries, ran to the child, stuck a finger in his throat and managed to extract the coin. When the father returned from work his wife told him what had happened, but "forgot" to note that it was my mother who had saved his son from certain death. My stepfather and mother were very fond of the child, who would enjoy entering their apartment, eating something and spending time with them despite his mother's objections. My mother and stepfather gave him what his parents would not. I hope that child remembers my mother and stepfather kindly.

The Bloodletter

During one visit with my mother, I had a special experience. I met a relatively older man who dealt in bloodletting using razor blades and ram horns. The man treated people who had high blood pressure, as was the custom back in Yemen.

Since my stepfather, who was usually an athletic and energetic man, suffered from chronic headaches (migraines) caused by high blood pressure, the bloodletter would arrive every six months. I was curious to see the treatment.

My stepfather sat in a chair with his back turned to the bloodletter. The bloodletter would shave the lower part of his neck, creating six or seven small cuts and pressing the hollow part of the horn to the wounds. Using his mouth, he would create suction to increase blood flow. This made the horn press against the wound, and every time the horn was full of blood he would release it, drain the blood into a special vessel and repeat the action several times. By the end of the treatment my stepfather felt considerable relief and was quite pleased.

Respecting the Dead

I can't remember my mother ever sitting listlessly, she was always looking for people to help, usually without reward. The Tassa family lived in the house across the street and had good neighborly relations with my mother and stepfather. When I would visit my mother's house, I would play soccer with their son Shmuel Tassa, along with Benyamin and Mordechai Shimoni and other friends. Over time we became a real soccer team called "The HaTikva Youths".

Shmuel's father was ill, and lay on his deathbed. His situation deteriorated to the point that they were certain he wouldn't see another sunrise. My mother told the family: "Go to bed and I will stay with your father." And so, at four in the morning the father passed away. My mother decided not to wake the family. She went down to the yard, brought dirt in a bucket, scattered it around the room and brought the corpse down to the floor on her own. Then she lit candles in his memory, spread oil on him as was the custom among the Jews of Yemen, and rubbed his hands and feet to keep them supple and prevent them from drying up. In the morning she woke the family and sadly informed them of the father's death.

When I heard this story I found it difficult to understand how my mother had the strength to face such tasks. It turned out she drew her strength from her faith in God. When someone claimed she was receiving some reward for her actions she would answer: "Whoever suspects the righteous will suffer." There were occasions when my mother was asked to treat people in exchange for payment, but the sum was minimal compared to the investment. She didn't care about the amount of money, but rather the privilege of treating those solitary people who were ignored even by those closest to them. Sometimes Mother had to sleep in their rooms and help them vacate themselves and bathe, despite their weight. She would cook for them, do their laundry, clean and care for them and feed them, patiently and compassionately. Those people she helped often made her promises and failed to keep them. She learned to trust God and hoped to receive her reward in Heaven, when her time came.

Pomegranate Shells and Shoe Soles Mixed in Henna

During one of my mother's visits to Kerem HaTemanim, an acquaintance told her of his daughter, who suffered from eczema in both hands. Every treatment, from the best professors, had failed, and the girl's father was at a loss. It turns out he had remarried and his wife cared little for her stepdaughter despite her illness. The girl was forbidden to touch cleaning materials but the stepmother utterly refused to accept this, and was generally displeased to have a daughter from whom she would receive no compensation. My mother, who had brought knowledge of natural remedies to medical problems from Yemen, including skin diseases, instructed the father to bring the girl to her for treatment, where she used henna, dry pomegranate shells and old shoe soles. The pomegranate shells and shoe soles were burnt to ashes, which she mixed with henna and a bit of water before massaging the ointment into the infected areas. The paste greatly irritated the skin and the girl had to restrain herself from scratching, which was not at all an easy thing to do. Day by day the bandages were replaced, and after forty days – "not thirty-nine or thirty-eight but precisely forty days," so said my mother, the girl was healed. The skin of her hands became healthy and smooth as a baby's.

When the stepmother learned that the treatment was complete and the girl had recovered she asked her to return home, but the girl refused and stayed with my mother for ten years, until she was old enough to live independently.

Change of Place, Change of Fortune

A solitary man, who seemed slightly odd, would stay with my mother and stepfather during Sabbath dinners. My stepfather, as my mother discovered after her marriage, was illiterate and knew little of the blessings. My mother had not learned them either, but had learned to read during her marriage to my biological father, who had been an exceptional student from early childhood. It was important to my mother to have someone who could perform the Kiddush properly, and bless the meal after eating.

After feasting to his heart's content, the guest would stay at the home of my mother and her husband, and tell stories that combined reality with a considerable amount of imagination. They enjoyed hearing the stories that "the Spirit of God" would invest in him, and would raise their spirits. Some time before the Six Day War the guest told them of what was about to happen, and even noted that the war would last six days and that Israel would defeat its enemies through angels that would fight alongside the soldiers of Israel.

It turned out the man was a rabbi situated in the depths of the Zohar and Kabbalah, who dealt with fates and fortunes, and would advise people on important matters.

The years passed and I built a family. After nineteen years of marriage and three children – Uriya, Yiftach and Yochemed – I separated from my first wife and moved in with my mother. At the time I was an assistant manager of the Inbal dance group and we were about to go on a two month tour of the United States. Since I was in deep crisis following my divorce I considered the phrase "Change of Place, Change of Fortune" and thought about living in America for a time, trying my luck there.

I told my mother and stepfather about my plans, but they were not thrilled and tried to convince me to return to Israel once the tour was over. My mother even made a promise: "Stay with us and we'll help you as much as we can." I explained to her that I could not find my place in Israel, and wanted to face new challenges, maybe fortune would smile on me. "Let's make a deal," Mother said, "I'll invite the rabbi to read your future." As I had always believed in my mother's healthy sensibilities, I agreed to her request.

A few days later the rabbi was waiting for me at my mother's house. When he heard of my wishes he asked for my name and surname, my mother's name and the date of my birth. He perused one of the books he'd brought with him and began saying things that surprised me. He said: "You work with people who listen to you…" and other things I thought only I knew. When I told him I was divorced with three children, he said after turning through the book: "I'm not surprised you were divorced. After looking through the book I can see you were not a good fit!" I felt that I could trust him. And then he asked me to turn my back to him and said: "I will open the second book and, without looking, place your finger on the page." I did as he asked. The book was covered in letters from Aleph to Taf. After I'd pointed to one of the letters, the rabbi took out another book where each letter had meaning and interpretation. The letter I'd pointed to meant "Wherever you go, you will succeed."

When my mother heard this she said: "Bon voyage, my boy, now I'm at peace. But know you have a place to return to."

This meeting gave me confidence, faith and hope, and when I stayed in America I felt I would succeed in general, and financially in particular, that I would be allowed to do my work unburdened by worry.

My Mother, Who Birthed Me

My mother, who birthed me
to you I give my thanks wholeheartedly
for my life and love
for my honor and glory

My mother, my only mother,
you are my light and pride
Please, my God, keep her safe for me
Because without her I am forlorn

Pure as the moon, smart as the sun $\Big\}2$
Clean as a dove loyal to God

Helping others was your calling
Any and all who asked
Whether it was friend or neighbor
Always in the spirit of the God in whom you believed

From dawn to dusk your watch held
With selfless generosity

With all your heart's love
Giving to all those in need

A noblewoman of many titles
Her heart and mouth were always at one $\Big\}2$

From your loving son Moshiko – 21/9/2005

Humility and Emotion – Grandfather Saadia Hasheishe

My grandfather Saadia Hasheishe was born in the city of Hasheishe in Yemen. He was a pleasant man, bright-faced, humble and shy. After the death of my grandmother – my mother's mother – my grandfather remarried several times. When he came to Israel he married a woman who had a son named Yechiel, and after her death he married Regina, who he loved deeply and was loved in return. Regina gave my grandfather a daughter and a son – Simcha and Yaakov – but for reasons I do not know she was unable to care for them, and they were given up to social services. My mother took care of Simcha and Yaakov as though they were her biological siblings.

The reader will probably not understand why my grandfather, Mori Saadia, would remarry so many times. It turned out the women he married were ill, mentally or physically, and needed someone to take care of them. More than once villagers would ask my grandfather why he chose these women, as he could have even the most beautiful woman. "If someone takes the most beautiful one, what will happen to the rest?" was his answer. My grandfather lived to help all those in need.

He worked as a gravedigger in the cemetery of Nahalat Yitzhak, and sadly, I did not have many opportunities to see him.

One day, returning from school to my grandmother's house, I was met with a locked door. I knocked on the door as hard as I could and my father, busy playing cards with his friends, opened the door a mere crack, held out a hand, took my backpack and whispered that Grandfather Saadia Hasheishe had passed away. He gave me several pennies and said: "Go to the funeral home at Hadasa Hospital, you'll find your mother there." Grandfather's funeral took place at the same cemetery where he worked – Nahalat Yitzhak. May his memory be a blessing.

My grandfather Saadia Hasheishe, with my mother at his side,
her brother Yechiel seated on her knee.
On the upper left is my mother's sister Shoshana,
on the right her cousin Naomi

Chapter 5

My Father – The Potential and Games of Chance

From the day I was born, I never felt my father's presence at home, nor do I remember ever getting a hug or a kiss from him. Unfortunately, my father spent more time outside the house than inside. I was nine months old when my mother divorced him and I was left in the care of his mother, my grandmother Badre. Father was a ladies' man, they loved him, his beautiful face and the color of his skin, and he was sadly drawn to that lifestyle which did him no favors and divested himself of all responsibilities.

And yet, as I grew older, I got to know the positive side of him, whether his religious education or his artistic talents. He knew how to entertain people and make them laugh, both within and beyond the family. I was charmed by him on holidays, especially Passover, when he would run the Seder in the custom of the Jews of Yemen.

My father, Shalom Yitzhak-Halevy

Though he was absent all throughout the year, Father knew that on Passover, on Sukkot, on Rosh HaShana and Yom Kippur he had to be with his family. We always waited for him, always nervous as to whether he would in fact come. He would never call ahead and let us know that he'd be arriving, it was always a surprise, and as he came so too would he leave.

After separating from my mother Father felt free, and less committed to me and my sister Bracha. I had no particular feelings towards him either, which saddened me because I couldn't learn all the positive things that were embedded in him.

When we were teenagers Father "married" a Polish woman named Rachel. She delivered his daughter Aviva. During World War II Father joined the British army and was drafted into the British Air Force, but during his service he began to smoke, drink and play cards. These three habits were his downfall.

His mental and financial state dwindled to almost nothing, and every time he ran out of money after a game of cards he would come to his mother's house, ask her for money and excuse it by claiming he had to undergo some surgery or other. My grandmother, who feared for him, would "scrape together" money from different places and as soon as she gave it to him Father's mood would improve dramatically.

I was angry at Father for acting this way, and angry at Grandmother for wanting to please him even though she knew he was lying directly to her face. To this Grandmother would reply: "Wait until you have children, we'll see how you handle it."

After fifteen years of marriage Rachel, Father's Polish wife, decided to divorce him. She left him and took her daughter Aviva with her. This saddened both my sister and I, but my grandmother took it hardest as she had loved Aviva very much. Aviva loved Grandmother no less – as well as her meals. She would visit my grandmother on Saturdays and enjoy the warm and delicious kubana (a traditional Yemenite dish) Grandmother made so well. After they left, Rachel demanded we have no further contact with them and never try to locate them.

My father continued his delinquency, bordering on criminal acts, and wandered from place to place. Anytime he felt someone was looking for him and the ground was getting too hot to handle, he would move to a new place.

After several years he married for a third time, this time to Mazal, a Turkish woman who bore him a son named Nechmad. This marriage ran aground as well. But he wasn't the only one to suffer from the separation; his disappearance and the shirking of his wife and son ruined Mazal's relationship with my grandmother, who would always pay the price for my father's behavior. I had to intervene more than once, sometimes physically, to protect my grandmother from Mazal. Once, after a violent altercation, I returned home late and from afar I could see a group of men sitting on the porch. I knew they were waiting to settle the score with me. I hid in the dark and when they were gone I entered my home. Unexpected visits from creditors, coming to demand money my father had lost in card games, was my lot in life as well. I was angry at Father and found it difficult to forgive him for what he'd done.

Only my sister and I remained in contact with him. His other two children, Aviva and Nechmad, wanted nothing to do with him.

Sometimes Father would attend my dance recitals or, on occasion, a soccer game, and would yell, cheer and encourage me with all his might. This amazed me a bit, but he was always doing his own thing, going wild when his favorite team won.

In 1973, my relationship with my father was severed due to my trip to America. I would often come to Israel and visit my children, but I never saw my father. When his health deteriorated – due to his smoking and drinking his lungs were utterly ruined – my sister alerted me from abroad. My sister couldn't stand hospitals and she was unable to visit him. I came to Israel, visited him at the hospital, and once the two of us were alone he asked me to forgive him for all the wrongs he'd done us. He knew his end was nigh. I approached the doctor treating him to ask about Father's condition. The doctor said he was far beyond healing.

A week after I returned to America, Father passed away.

My father, Shalom Yitzhak-Halevy, was buried next to his brother (by his biological father, but with a different mother) Haim Yitzhak-Halevy, who died a week before him. The two had not been in contact for years. On the day of Father's funeral, so I was told, Haim's children had just finished sitting shiva for their father. They came to the memorial at the cemetery in Holon and ran into my family as they were holding my father's funeral. It turned out the hand of

Fate had arranged things just so, as my father's grave was dug right next to his brother's. Since then, whenever Haim's children visit their father's grave, they say Kaddish for my father as well. Perhaps my father did something good that merited this. May his memory be a blessing!

Searching for Aviva

After Aviva and her mother left our house, we honored their wish not to look for them. They had vanished without a trace anyway, but that didn't stop us from thinking about Aviva throughout the years and missing her. The older I grew the more powerful my curiosity became. As an instructor and choreographer of folk dances I was invited to teach in every city in Israel and would always look for her face in the crowd. Sometimes I would dare to approach someone and ask if her name happened to be Aviva. It would happen on the bus, the train or even in the street, and though I never found her, I never lost hope. More than once I thought that perhaps Aviva's mother had returned to Poland and taken Aviva with her, but even that thought could not deter me from the hope that someday I would find my sister.

Once, during a meeting with my father, I told him that I was searching for Aviva. He told me that once, while delivering bread on behalf of Achdut Bakery in the Krayot area to grocery stores in the Haifa region, he saw his ex-wife Rachel leaving one of the stores in Hadar. My father spoke with the grocer, who he knew well, and asked if the woman's name was Rachel. The grocer replied in the affirmative. My father asked if Rachel's daughter was named Aviva, and the grocer again said yes.

My father's story gave me hope. As an instructor for the Druze dance troupe in the village of Osafiya, I would visit the area once a week. I scheduled a meeting with my father by that same grocery store in Hadar. My father went into the store and asked the grocer how he could track down Aviva. The grocer, surprised by the question, asked Father what he had to do with her. My father could no longer hide his secret and revealed to the grocer that he was her father. The grocer was very excited and said that his wife and Aviva had their hair cut by the same barber. He gave my father the barber shop's address.

I received the address from my father and drove there. The owner thought I had come for a haircut, but I quickly told him I was Aviva's brother and that I'd heard she was his client. I added that I had been searching for her for many years. The barber was very moved and told me that Aviva was like an adoptive daughter for him and his wife. He immediately went to the phone and called her. Her reaction was chilly and she was about to hang up. I took the receiver from the barber's hand and told Aviva I very much wanted to meet her, and afterwards she could decide whether or not to continue the relationship.

Aviva gave me her address and asked me to hurry because she was on her lunch break at work. I did the best I could and made it to her. The atmosphere was cool. We barely shook hands. This was not how I imagined my first meeting with my sister after twenty-five years.

I felt that Aviva mistrusted me, and indeed, she had called her husband who worked at the Zim offices in Haifa Port. In the meantime, we sat and talked. I showed her pictures I'd received from my sister Bracha of the two of them on Tel-Aviv's promenade, with Bracha protecting Aviva.

Aviva was similarly restrained at the sight of the photos. She asked many questions, as was appropriate for a head secretary at a well-known law office in Haifa. Her first question was where my father and her mother had married. I promised to give her an answer at our next meeting. All this time my father waited in the street. Aviva refused to see him.

The wedding, so my father told me, was at the Petach Tikva Rabbinate. The very next day I went to Petach Tikva's Rabbinate offices, asking for a copy of the marriage certificate. My request was denied. I was told the Rabbinate no longer held the old certificates. Suddenly one of the rabbis approached me and said that the Rabbinate's yard had several sacks intended for the incinerator, perhaps one of them held the certificate. I didn't hesitate, and went out into the yard, digging through the bags. To my surprise, after two or three hours I found the certificate.

At our next meeting I showed Aviva the certificate, but she still held back from opening up to me; on the contrary, she was upset that she had no birth certificate. Here as well I asked my father where Aviva was born, and with the details I received from him I went to the Ministry of the Interior in Jerusalem. I found her birth certificate there.

By our third meeting, Aviva understood that there was no way around accepting the fact that I was her brother. To my surprise she began to pull out copies of those same photographs I'd brought during my previous visit, as well as the marriage certificate I had worked to find. I understood that she had in fact been testing me.

Then Aviva began telling me about her life, how disappointed she had been on multiple occasions when people had deceived her. She said her mother had never told her who her father was, and some spread rumors that her father was an Arab.

After setting things straight between us, I asked to bring along my sister Bracha to our next meeting. Since then Bracha, Aviva and I get together every now and then. To the day he died, my father never received any attention from his children Aviva and Nechmad.

And Another Small Story

During my search for Aviva I spent a few months teaching a workshop for folk dance instructors at a studio on Arlozorov Street in Haifa. Many were the guests who came to my workshop, including former Head of the Shin Bet Yaakov Peri, as well as Yonatan Gabai, a dance choreographer in Israel and one of the most active in the Haifa region for anything pertaining to folk dances. Efi Netzer accompanied my lessons on the accordion. After the workshop Efi Netzer would play "Debka Uriya", the first dance I composed, and we would join him. The group of students included a Yemenite girl named Bat-Sheva, who later turned out to be a good friend of my sister Aviva. Bat-Sheva even tried to convince Aviva to come with her to the studio, if only to see the cute Yemenite instructor…

In the meantime, I had gotten married, and lived in the home of my wife's parents in Kerem HaTeimanim. The neighbor who lived next door was named Selma. After a brief acquaintance it turned out Selma had a niece named Bat-Sheva who would visit her every now and then with her good friend Aviva. Over time Bat-Sheva told me that Aviva, who was unaware of her Yemenite roots, loved Aunt Selma's kubana and jachnun. She didn't understand why she was so compelled by Yemenite food. After we met, and her Yemenite roots were clear to her, I revealed she had more Yemen in her than Poland. She also greatly resembled Grandmother Badre.

Aviva is married today to Yaakov Levy, and is a mother to twins, Shai and Doron, born after a long wait. Doron has been living in America for years, but

I managed to attend his wedding before he left; Shai has a law degree from the Hebrew University. He is a teacher and tests law students at the University, and is considered among the best in his profession.

A Eulogy for Mother

My mother, may her memory be a blessing, lived to the age of ninety-four. She passed away in 2008, and this is the eulogy I read over her grave at the funeral:

Dear Mother,
You have finally attained peace
From childhood you were your parents' firstborn
And took upon yourself the burden of heaven
To be responsible for your brother and sisters.

When you turned fourteen
You married for the first time
and by sixteen you were already mother
to my sister and then to me
Unfortunately, your marriage didn't last
and we were kept from being with you.

And in the meantime we grew up, and you remarried.
You were a beautiful woman
and when you were troubled by suitors
You realized "it is unwise for a woman to be alone
only a married woman avoids harassment."
Forty years you lived with him
Your life was not a garden of roses
but you kept on, with some grinding of teeth,
believing it was the decree of heaven.

You dedicated those difficult days to good deeds for the needy,
nights and days without recompense, you gave those people faith
and used any means to restore their personal dignity.
You made matches free of charge, always finding the right lid for the pot.

How proud and satisfied you were to see couples like those,
who had lost almost all hope, and now were starting proper families.
In houses of mourning you would lament, cook and help.
You were gone from home, sometimes for days at a time,
to aid the desolate ill on their last legs.

At the end of every visit you would walk me to the bus station
and proudly tell people I was your son
And they would tell you: "You have a righteous mother
whose blessings come true."

Rabbi Yosef Tzubari, may his memory be a blessing, knew of your sainted acts
and told you once that you would be allowed into heaven with your clothes
and since Rabbi Tzubari is already "there", he will certainly vouch for you.
You always believed that "the emissaries of good deeds are not harmed"
but more than once your kindness was repaid with cruelty
and even physical injuries that confined you to your bed,
but you stubbornly held onto your faith.

After forty years of marriage your second husband died of a wasting illness,
our stepfather Saadia,
and again you were free to continue your contribution, all the more vigorously.
Your house was so full you could barely make your way to bed
but this did not trouble you
and nothing could compare to that same satisfaction
of giving someone the thing they needed.

Years passed since the death of your second husband
You felt lonely and began considering the possibility of a third marriage
To have a friend, a companion
You were worried that your children had their own families
and would have no time to see to your needs
I understood and encouraged you, but my sister was less thrilled
and was ultimately convinced despite herself, and you married
for the third time.

It was my sister upon whom the burden fell of seeing to your needs.
One day you broke your pelvis, were hospitalized
and underwent hip replacement surgery.
After a few months of recovery you fell on your face at home and injured your nose.
We understood we had to find a proper home that could care for and serve you.
We tried to see to your every need.
And you loved the "Parents Together 2" house, who went above and beyond for you.
You had only kind words for the therapists and the nurses
for the dedicated and warm treatment they gave you,
you finally felt, after so many years of serving others,
what it was like to be served.

Before we part ways, I want to tell you
that I will miss your blessings that so empowered me wherever I went,
whatever I did, whenever I succeeded, thank God.
And you, Mother, keep sending us your blessings from on high
to your children, grandchildren, great-grandchildren and on down,
who loved you and you them,
for whom you were a special woman.
I promise to visit you and say "Kaddish" because you deserve it
and to maintain the connection in the manner of Jewish tradition.

May you rest in peace

Part B: Dance Steps

My modern dance in Naomi Aleskovsky's dance company

Chapter 1
⊚⊚⊚⊚⊚⊚⊚⊚ ⊚⊚⊚⊚⊚⊚⊚

The Women and Men in my Professional World

In 1949 I had to leave Givot Zayid and return to Tel-Aviv to help my grandmother, who had been left on her own after my sister, who had been staying with her until then, married and moved away with her husband. I asked the kibbutz to let me take a year-long sabbatical, and made my way to the city I was not overly fond of, for the reasons that had caused me to leave in the first place, and to Givot Moshe Aleph which I actually did love.

The day after my arrival I was hired at a toy factory, with only a fence separating it from my grandmother's house. In the factory, managed by the **Brothers Dov and Imrei**, there were two sections. In one the men used chiseling machines to make wooden soldiers, domino cubes, beads for abaci and more; in the other section the women hand-painted the materials passed to them from the male wing. **Chana Eliazov** was the work director at the factory.

Chana Eliazov – First Opportunity

Chana Eliazov – a famous ballet dancer and head dancer of the Israeli Opera – was forced to leave the dance profession after she married, at the peak of her success, and find another source of income. You could feel that Chana's body was at work, but her soul remained hovering somewhere in the world of dance.

I, who even in the kibbutz days loved to dance, entertain and sing, also did my work while singing and dancing. At the factory, as I would pass the raw materials to the women's section, I would improvise all sorts of dance moves while in close contact with the chiseling machine, jumping on worktables like the star of a Hollywood musical.

Chana Eliazov would follow my behavior, and one day she asked me: "How long are you planning to jump on tables and waste your talent for nothing, don't you want to dance professionally?"

I was only seventeen, too innocent to fully understand what she meant, and yet

I said yes anyway. Chana promised that someday soon she would take me to the school where she'd started dancing. I waited with great anticipation for that day to come.

We came to **Mia Arbatova's** dance school and were greeted with great warmth, especially Chana. Mia, and everyone who knew and remembered Chana from her glory days, were pleased by her visit. I was presented to Mia as someone interested at trying their luck in the field of dance.

Mia Arbatova, the Woman Who Made Me a Dancer

Of the dozens who danced at the studio there were only three men – the veteran of the group **Yitzchak Mashiach**, **Zvi Glazer** and **Moshe Lazare**. At the time there was not nearly enough awareness among men about the field of ballet dance, this being the reason there were so few male dancers. I was the fourth and Mia gave me personal attention and assisted me with everything. At the end of one of the lessons she suggested that I could come to the studio any time I wanted, for as long as my strength held out. I would go to the studio and practice ballet dance techniques from three o'clock, as soon as the working day was done, until ten at night, and I would return home exhausted but utterly satisfied.

After two months I thought I would have to stop dancing. Most of my income was dedicated to supporting my grandmother and maintaining the house, I didn't have enough to cover the high monthly expense of dance classes. I spoke about it with Mia, who understood my problem but pleaded with me to continue coming to the studio, even for free, so long as I didn't stop dancing.

After three months in which I made huge advances in the field of dance, I joined the Mia Arbatova School's dance company. It was a huge compliment to me, an advancement and future challenge.

Today, 65 years after making my first step into the world of dance, and in light of my past achievements as a dancer and choreographer, I am grateful to Chana Eliazov for her esteemed part in my advancement and successes.

Mia Arbatova's school was practically the authority on anything pertaining to classical ballet and ethnic dances originating in the Soviet Union. Mia knew how to get the absolute best out of each and every student. She did much to get to know her dancers to their cores, each with their unique characteristics and special sensitivities, before assigning them any particular role. She knew how to get the absolute maximum out of each and every one of us, especially the male dancers who excelled with their high technical abilities.

Mia Arbatova, my ballet teacher

And indeed, dancers who had spent several years at her school radiated self-confidence and personality. Mia trained hundreds of dancers, among them those who would later be accepted to professional dance companies in the United States and Europe. Even those who remained in Israel, some of whom opened dance schools of their own, maintained the same attitude and seriousness that characterized Mia.

As someone counted among her students for six years, and as her practice partner in lessons, I absorbed the special qualities of Mia Arbatova's personality, and I owe her a tremendous debt for granting me the basics and molding my personality. It is because of her that I became a professional dance teacher and choreographer.

Mia Arbatova and Mia Pick

In the meantime, I was conscripted into the army and, due to my artistic talents, I was assigned to military dance companies – for the first six months in the Carmel dance company and later in the dance squad. After my discharge I appeared at the "Li-La-Lo" and "Do-Re-Mi" theaters as a dancer in musical plays, and I was invited to join dancer and choreographer **Naomi Aleskovsky** as an understudy of famous dancer and choreographer **Yonatan Karmon**, who quit in order to establish "The Karmon Dance company".

Mia Arbatova's Sailor Dance

The Dancers of Mia Arbatova

My gleeful leap at the Yama Beach in Tel-Aviv

On the beach of Tel Aviv with Mia Arbatova

Me with the dancer Zohara on the beach

Me with the dancer Bruria on the beach (both nieces of Mia Arbatova)

Me with the quizmaster Shmuel Rozen

Me and Shmuel Rosen the quizman

Jerome (Jerry) Robbins – A World-Class Professional with Personal Charm

I had the pleasure and honor of meeting famous choreographer Jerome Robbins during his first visit to Israel in 1953. Robbins had come at the invitation of the American/Israeli Cultural Fund, to get a close and personal impression of the level Israeli dance was currently at, and how it was developing. At the same time Robbins was teaching a class for the senior dancers, all of whom had been carefully selected.

I was fortunate to be one of the four male dancers chosen to participate in this course. There were three of us from Mia Arbatova's studio, and one from Gertrude Kraus' studio. Most of the female dancers were also from Mia Arbatova's studio.

The course, which lasted three weeks, was based on one of Jerome Robbins' successful choreographed pieces, InterPlay. It was a challenge for me, and I was pleased to meet the demands of the renowned choreographer.

A party in honor of Jerome Robbins, second from the left

Robbins' reputation preceded him as one of the top choreographers in the world, in works such as "West Side Story", "The King and I", "The Cage" and more.

Thanks to his works he was recognized as one of the great choreographers who influenced global dance.

Once, after rehearsals, Robbins approached me and asked whether I was of Yemenite descent. When I said yes, he said "What are you doing here then, why aren't you joining the Inbal dance company?" I told him that Inbal had only just started up and I was interested in challenges, in light of my technical achievements in the field of classic and modern dance. I told him: "I can do four pirouettes on one leg, two in the air and I land on my knee like a feather – you want me to shift to Yemenite dance? It's like going backwards." But Robbins saw things differently. He saw in Inbal's dance theater a unique artistic revelation in terms of the methods and style of its work and believed in that in the near future it would be known throughout the world.

I am thankful I had the honor of working with Robbins and absorbing some of his professional knowledge and personal advice. A few months later I found myself in the Inbal dance company.

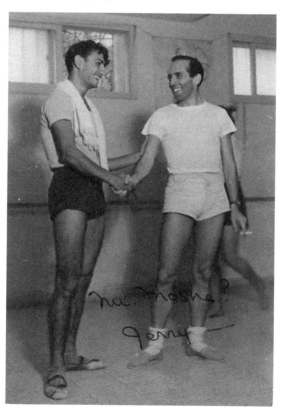

Me with Jerome Robbins

Sara Levy-Tanai – The Founder of "Inbal"

Joining Inbal as a dancer revealed a world I had not previously been aware of. It was 1953. After six years of classic ballet, modern dance, jazz, tap-dancing and different character dances, with a high technical aptitude that any dancer would be proud of, I began working in a style of dance with more emotional content than technical. I met Sara Levy-Tanai – quite a name in the world of dance.

After struggling to make the most of her artistic potential in one of the Israeli theaters, without much success, Sara decided to establish an artistic framework within which she could express her artistic, cultural, Biblical and Jewish wishes. For this purpose, she began gathering boys and girls of Yemenite descent who were convinced to drop everything and dedicate themselves to fulfilling her dream. Aided and supported by the HaPoel Committee of the Histadrut, Sara's students began working in small groups, with no prior experience in the field of dance but with a powerful adventurous spirit. Thus, was the Inbal dance company born. Sara's first works with the dance company were based on the Israeli pastoral, such as shepherds' dances, sheep games, Biblical sets, Jacob and Esau and "Transit Camp School".

Anyone watching the dance company felt a new and fresh wind breezing through the field of dance. Fate smiled on Sara and her dance company, but to implement all her plans a larger budget was needed that the Histadrut could not provide. Sara began looking for other financial benefactors who could set up the funds needed to develop the dance company and promise Inbal some peace of mind.

The organization that took it upon itself to sponsor the Inbal dance company was the American Israeli Cultural Fund. This organization granted Sara and the dance company members financial security and an absence of concerns. This period generated the works "Shabbat Shalom", "The Song of Deborah", "Queen of Sheba", "Desert" and other works of choreography that grew Inbal from a dance company to a dance theater.

Sara Levy-Tanai's dream was to develop a new language of dance influenced by the ethnic origins of the different populations in Israel, but her main emphasis was on Yemenite culture and its legacy.

שרה לוי־תנאי

בת לעולי־תימן, ילידת ירושלים. סיימה את בית־המדרש
למורים ולגננות ע״ש לוינסקי. עבדה כגננת במשך 15 שנים
בת״א ובקיבוץ רמת־הכובש. בתקופה זו ביימה הצגות
רבות בבתי־ספר ובחברות נוער, ניהלה חגיגות ומסכתות
רבות־משתתפים בקיבוצים, הדריכה גננות ומורות בשירים,
חיברה שירים ולחנים רבים. את „ענבל" ייסדה בשנת
1949, ומאז הינה הבמאית, הכוריאוגרפית ומנהלת
התיאטרון. כן חיברה ועיבדה שרה לוי־תנאי רבים מן
הלחנים והשירים המופיעים ברפרטואר התיאטרון. שרה
לוי־תנאי היא כלת פרס „אנגל" להלחנת שירי־עם, מטעם
עירית ת״א; זכתה בפרס אהרונוביץ מטעם ההסתדרות
על יצירתה ועבודתה ב„ענבל" וזכתה בתואר „הכוריאוגרף
הטוב ביותר לשנת 1962", בפסטיבל תיאטרון האומות
בפאריס.

Sara Levy-Tanai: Daughter of Yemenite immigrants, born in Jerusalem. Graduated from the Levinsky Beit Midrash for Kindergarten and School Teachers. Worked as a kindergarten teacher for 15 years in Tel-Aviv and Kibbutz Ramat HaKovesh. During this period, she directed many performances in schools and youth groups, managed festivities and revues in the kibbutzim, taught songs to kindergarten and school teachers, and composed many songs and melodies. She founded Inbal in 1949, and has since served as director, choreographer and manager of the theater. Sara Levy-Tanai also composed and arranged many of the melodies and songs that appear in the theater repertoire. Sara Levy-Tanai is an Angel Award recipient for her folk song compositions, granted on behalf of Tel-Aviv City Hall; a recipient of the Aharonovitch Award on behalf of the Histadrut for her creation and work in Inbal, and was named Best Choreographer of 1962 at the Theater of Nations Festival in Paris.

Me with Sara Levy-Tanai on the roof of my house

Me with Sara Levy-Tanai and Meir Ovadia at a train station in England

A Dancer in Inbal

I personally had no problem managing with the new style, though I was not used to it, but I felt somewhat disappointed at the poor technical level compared to the demands of the Mia Arbatova school. Sara Levy-Tanai took note of my abilities and skills as a dancer and assigned me primary roles but rehearsing the dance moves felt somewhat sickening. Searching for the step, the motion, the combination between the two, until the whole picture was completed, wasted precious time. Even when the piece was completed, it was difficult to say with any confidence that it would not be changed the next day. This phenomenon repeated itself again and again, so that even mere minutes before taking the stage Sara might change a large part of a dancer's role, after weeks and months of rehearsal.

Margalit Oved, Queen of Sheba. Meir Ovadia and me as the Queen's guards

Sara's perfectionism often brought about the opposite result. Dancers with professional backgrounds would find it difficult to adapt themselves to this kind of work. On the other hand, inexperienced dancers accepted this innocently, due to their lack of professional experience.

After four years of work with Inbal it was hard for me to accept the fact that we had no technical classes on a proper professional level to train our dancers' bodies and warm them up prior to rehearsals. I started considering whether I would leave. For some reason Sara had strong objections to the techniques of classical ballet, as she believed this technique would interfere with her dancers' ability to express themselves in the "Inbal style". I believed this was a mistake, and some months later, after being persuaded by Jerome Robbins – one of Sara's idols as an artist and choreographer – she changed her mind. Robbins explained to her the importance of classical ballet technique in improving a dancer's capabilities, regardless of the style of dance they were using.

Another reason I wanted to quit the dance company was the pace of study and rehearsals. Every chorographical subject took between eight months and a year of work. So many attempts, so many changes, so much searching for the right step and move. Sara Levy-Tanai lacked the correct professional tools to implement her ideas, and it was her lack of professional experience that caused a lack in her self-confidence and her many failed attempts during her work. She needed dancers who would assist her in finding the right move. More than once she hit a dead end and her stress would bring the pace of progress through a choreographed work to a complete standstill.

I myself was asked more than once to step out into the studio hall in order to improvise movements and steps that would help continue the choreographic work. While I was happy to feel like I was an active partner in the creative work, it was hard for me to accept this method.

Yisha'aya Tzafri, me, Avshalom Sela, Chana Minzili and Shoshana Tovi, members of Inbal

Me in the role of the Queen's guard

Chana Mizeli and me

From "Nights of Canaan"

Yudaleh Cohen and me in a midnight prayer show

Inbal dancers in a scene from "Desert"

I offer a chicken in the Inbal dance

With Golda Meir after a show

The Inbal dance company traveling in England

Performing in the Kibbutzim

During the holidays, the Inbal dance company would make a series of performances in the kibbutzim. On one of those days, during the lunch break, Sara said that due to budget concerns the dance company would have to split in two in order to perform in two kibbutzim simultaneously, and adapt our dances to the number of dancers in each location. When she assigned their roles, some bitterness arose among the dance company members, who said they were tired of repeating the same pieces over and over. Sara was furious and said that "Swan Lake" was repeatedly performed as well, and no one was tired of that. Here too I could not agree with the comparison, especially as this was a program for kibbutzim that, by all accounts, should be light and simple. When she noticed that the dancers did not agree with her, Sara threw a petty question out: "Is anyone willing to work on new material?" The answer was not long in coming. One of the dance company members shouted "Yes!" It was **Tzefion Atzta**, z"l – one of the talented musicians in Inbal – but when Sara turned her gaze to him, he pointed at me and said: "Moshiko's up for it." I was shocked! In a split-second so many thoughts crossed my mind, but I came to one conclusion: if my answer were no, I would be denied a golden opportunity to prove my skills at choreography. So, Sara turned to me and asked: "Are you ready?" My answer was affirmative, and the idea became reality.

Dances and Shepherd's Games in the Inbal dance company

I was given my choreography work hours. The dance company members helped me complete the task. I fondly recall Chana Minzili, z"l, a dance company member who encouraged me and protected my work from any argument with Sara. I called my choreography "Debka Knaan" – a dance that incorporated men and women using the shepherd's game style of dance.

When the dance company went to perform at the kibbutzim my choreography was wildly successful and there were requests for encores after every show. Sara, who was with the dance company's second team, heard from my friends in the group about the success of "Debka Knaan". They suggested that in light of my debka's success, it should be the finale. Sara refused the suggestion and only allowed "Debka Knaan" to end the first part of the program.

The success of my choreography caught Sara's attention, and she asked to speak with me. She said she was pleased with my work and saw my progress as a natural process. In light of this, she suggested I would be given the light parts, so she could turn her full attention to bigger programs and ideas. I told Sara I was happy for the offer and hoped for more opportunities to prove my talents.

Months passed and nothing was done. Again, I felt a lack of interest in continuing with Inbal. I explained to Sara and the dance company members that I felt like a ripe fruit fallen from the tree, hungry for creative challenges. Sara heard my words and snickered, forgetting that once she hungered for meaningful work and sought any way to implement her wishes. With no option left to me, I decided to make good on my wishes and leave the dance company.

Upon leaving Inbal I began teaching private lessons to tap dancers, and when I saw that the number of my dancers had grown, I decided to open a school for jazz and tap, the first of its kind in Israel.

But within six months Sara asked me to return to Inbal, to prepare for the dance company's tour across Europe and the United States. Sara Levy-Tanai knew that as I knew all the parts, she wouldn't need to turn to another dancer. It was a heavy temptation, and I couldn't refuse the offer. I had to close my school, much to the disappointment of my students, and I returned to Inbal.

The Inbal dance company at the United Nations

The Inbal dance company in Philadelphia. Sara Levy-Tanai received the key to the city from the Mayor of Philadelphia

The Inbal dance company in the hall of the Security Council

The Inbal dance company after the performance, with guests

A Hora dance with the pantomime artist Marcel Marceau

With the Mayor of New York at City Hall

היום הולכים ל„ענבל"

מאת שולמית איתן

ה יום אנחנו הולכים ל„ענבל"! — הכריזה האם בארוחת הצהרים בקול עלי.

— ענבל? מה זה „ענבל"? — שאל אבנר בן השמונה.

— זה בטח שם של הצגה חדשה! — פסקה סמדר הבכורה.

סמדר בת השתים־עשרה היתיבה להכיר את אמה. אם אמא מבשרת בשמחה כזאת, הרי זו בודאי יציאה משותפת לתיאטרון או איזה הופעה!

רבות מחברותיה של סמדר אינן ששות כלל לצאת לבלות עם הוריהן. אבל עם אבא ואמא שלה, מדגישה סמדר, זה... „אחרת": משוחחים, מתכוננים, מתלבשים יפה ונוסעים יחד, בערב, כמו הגדולים. ושם, באולם, יושבים בשקט ומקשיבים... כי יודעים מראש שאחר כך, בדרך הביתה וגם בהפסקות, ידברו, ישאלו שאלות... ובאמצע אין שואלים דבר! רק אמא מתכופפת לפעמים ולוחשת מלת־הסבר הכרחית.

— אז תגידי כבר, מה זה? — מפציר אבנר.

— „ענבל" — אומרת אמא — זהו תיאטרון־מחול!

— ניחשתי נכון — מתגאה סמדר.

— נכון ולא נכון! — צוחקת אמא — זהו תיאטרון „מחול"! ולכל אחת משתי המלים הללו ערך ומשמעות. כשהלהקה קוראת שם לעצמה, הרי היא בוחרת את המלים בזהירות ובקפדנות. אבנר וסמדר הניחו מידיהם את הסכו"ם. השעינו עצמם אל מסעד הכיסא ונעצו באמם מבט מצפה. הם ידעו כי מיד יבואו דבריה. ואכן היא המשיכה:

— תיאטרון מעלה הצגות. הצגות שבהן יש תוכן ועלילה המסופרים לנו ע"י השחקנים. להקת־מחול, לעומת זאת, מר־פיעה לעתים בריקודי תנועה וקצב שאינם מלווים דיבור ואין בהם תוכן סיפורי. חברי „ענבל" מגישים גם קטעי ריקוד טהור וגם קטעי־משחק, בעיקר סביב סיפורי־חתנ״ך או הפולקלור התימני.

— איך אמרת „פולקלור"? — שאל אבנר.

— למה דוקא „תימני"? — הקשתה סמדר.

— אני שאלתי קודם! — התרעם אבנר.

האם הגישה את צלחיות הלפתן — הנה! אכלו בנחת ואני אספר לכם ואענה לשניכם גם יחד. „ענבל" זוהי להקה של צעירים וצעירות שעשמו להם למטרה למסור את הווי הארץ בתנועה, בזמר, במחול ובסיפור. והואיל והם עצמם, וכן ההנהלה והמדריכה של הלהקה, הנם בני תימן, ברור שהם עושים זאת בסגנון משלהם: הם שומרים על חן הדיבור וחרוזות התנועה של יהודי תימן ומעבדים אותם לריקוד ומשחק, כפי שתראו זאת בעצמכם.

הילדים סיימו בשקט את ארוחתם. שניהם חשבו על מה שיסופר להם וניסו לתאר לעצמם את מה שיראו. אבנר הסיר את הכלים מן השולחן וסמדר עזרה לאם בגיגוב והנה הפטירה האם כבדרך אגב:

כיצד יכינו הורים את ילדיהם לביקור מש...
תף בתיאטרון? כיצד יעוררו את סקרנותם למת־
רחש בעולם האמנות?

אנו מגישים הפעם נסיון־המחשה לשיחה
שהיא בבחינת גירוי־מעורר, סיפוק ידיעות וחכ־
וונה תרבותית, — בין הורים לילדיהם.
כמובן, יש להתאים את השיחה לגיל הילדים,
לתפיסתם ולהיעניינותם־לנושא, ע"י צמצום הסעיפים
השונים או הרחבתם והעמקתם.

— ובכן זכרו! הערב הולכים ללהקתה של שרה לוי ועד
אז עליכם לגמור שיעוריכם ולהסתפק לנוח היטב!

— „שרה לוי" — לחשה סמדר לעצמה — איפה שמעתי
את השם הזה?... ובקול אמרה: אני בטוחה שראיתי פעם את
שמה כתוב בעיתון. ופתאום פרצה בצחוק.

— אמא! הרי היום למדנו שיר מאת שרה לוי, בשיעור
לזמרה!

— באמת? — שאל אבנר. — איזה שיר?

— „עם השחר, עם האור / נעלה בהר המור" — פצחה
סמדר בקול רם ערב — וחוץ מזה המורה סיפר לנו שהיא חיברה
גם את „עלי באר" ו„אל גנת אגוז"!

— נכון! אמרה האם. — לפני שעמדה שרה לוי בראש
להקת „ענבל" היתה גננת ומחנכת במשך שנים רבות, ובשנים
אלה כתבה חיברה מגינונות להרבה הרבה
שירי ילדים. למשל: „קול דודי", המוכר לכם כל כך, ו„ליצן
קטן ונחמד" האהוב עליכם. „פרי גני" ו„אל תכה — לא נאה"...
והעיקר הוא, שלכל השירים הגיעה בכוחות עצמה...

— מניין את יודעת את כל זה, אמא? — שאל לפתע
אבנר.

— גם לי סיפרו! — ענתה האם — גם אני אוהבת לשאול
ולשמוע.

✳

בעת ההצגה ישבו הילדים דרוכים. עיניהם ליוו את תנו־
עותיהם החיננות של צוות־הרקדנים ואזניהם היו נטויות
לשירה הנאה וללמלל.

— ראיתם אילו בגדים יפים לובשת הכלה בתימן —
אמרה סמדר כתום החלק הראשון — „מן המקורות".

בחלק זה הדגימה וביארה שרה לוי, בעזרת חברי להקתה,
כיצד השתמשה בלבוש התימני המקורי התאימה אותו ע"י
עיבוד וסגנון לדרישות הבמה.

— הבגדים באמת מרהיבי־עין, — אמרה האם — אך
המעניין ביותר הוא שראיתם איך יוצרים את סגנון הלבוש
על הבמה. היתה זאת הזדמנות נדירה בשבילכם לראות איך
מעבירים את „החיים" אל „הבמה"!

— אני נהניתי ביותר בעיקר מסיפורו של התימני הזקן, המזמין
את רעיו להתונה! נזכר אבנר בחיוך.

— זה לא „סתם להצחיק" אבנר! — אמרה אמא — גם
קטע זה שולב בתוכנית כדי להראות את הקשר בין הדיבור
המזרחי היום־יומי, המלווה תנועות לרוב, ובין המחול על

תמונה מ"סעי, יונה" — משה לוי וחנה מיכזלי

הבמה. — דרך אגב, השמתם לב לדבריה של מנהלת הלהקה,
שאמרה כי... "הרוסי רוקד בתנועות רחבות... יש לו אדמה
תחת רגליו לרוב... ואילו התימני, בלחץ הגלוה, בין הכתלים
הגבוהים הסוגרים על הרחובות הצרים, מרקד כלפי מעלה...
כאילו הוא מנסה בריקודיו לעלות למרום... או לאמר תפילה...״?

— אני חושבת שב..."דעסה" ראינו "תנועה סתורה", כמו
שהסברת לנו בבית. — אמרה סמדר לאמה לאחר החלק
השני. — כי לא היה פה למעשה כל סיפור או עלילה.
האם היסה רגע:

— אינני יודעת עד כדי לפסוק — ענתה — אבל לי
נדמה שהתרגשת המדבר והצמאון האופפת את הקטע, ההילוך
הכבד והחדגווני המזכיר את הילוך הגמלים — הנם כאילו
תמונה מסופרת!

אבנר האזין בהנאה לשירים "מולדתי" ו"אל הרהט" המו־
כרים לו היטב, ובעיקר התרשם מן הכלי החדש שראה שם —
ה"ג'אנג'י". לבקשתו מאמו שתסביר לו את מבנה הכלי וקר־
א לויתיו אמרה האם: "הנה אבנרי משהו שאמא איננה יודעת,
ואני מציעה לך לשוח על כך מורתך לחליל"! ואבנר קיבל
את הצעתה.

בחלק השלישי צחקו הילדים למעט למשמע "דו־
שיח חלילים".

— הביטי אמא — קרא אבנר — הם כאילו רבים זה עם
זה בחלילים שלהם. אחד שואל, השני עונה; אחד רוגז, השני
צוחק...

— זה קצת כמו שאנחנו לומדים כעת בזמרה — אמרה
סמדר — על "שאלה" ו"תשובה" במוסיקה. גם ב"סעי, יונה"!
היו "שאלות ותשובות" בין העולם והעלמה. ("סעי, יונה"!
הוא מחול גועגועים ותרפפות).

— השוואתך יפה מאוד! — אמרה האם לבתה.

— "סעי, יונה"! — זה סתם משעמם! — אמר אבנר.

סמדר חייכה אל אמא וזו השיבה לה בחיוך: אה, סוד.
סמדר כבר "נערה" ואילו אבנרי עודני "ילד קטן" שאינו יכול
עדיין להבין תמונות כאלו של גועגועים והתבוששות וליהנות
מהן...

— כל אחד נהנה מן הקרוב אליו! — הסבירה האם לבנה.

— ואתה עודך קטן במקצת מכדי ליהנות מכל הקטעים. אני,
למשל, המוסיקה — נהניתי מהתמונה "נשים", כי כל תנועי־
תיהן כה קרובות לעבודתי במטבח ובמשק־הבית.

— ואני נהניתי בעיקר מ... — החל אבנר.

— יעקב ועשו — ניחשו אמא וסמדר יחדיו. הן זה עתה
למד זאת בבית־הספר והנה נזדמן לו לראות את "שיחת יעקב
עם עשו השב מצידו" — בחיניניות כזו על הבמה. כאן ראו
הילדים כיצד נוטלים סיפור־עלילה מן התנ"ך והופכים אותו
לתמונה חיה ועליזה ב"תיאטרון־מחול".

בדרך הביתה כבר לא היה צורך לאם לדרבן את הילדים
לשיחה. כשהם עומדים וממתינים לאוטובוס כבר ניסו השנים
כוחם בזכירת הדו־שיח מלא־החן וההומור שבין יעקב לעשו
השב מצידו, כשהם מהנים מפסוקיה של שרה לוי את
כל העומדים לידם. סמדר היתה יעקב ואבנר הצעיר דוקא
הוא היה עשו הבכור.

העלאת הרשמים והשאלות נמשכה גם לאחר מכן. כל
אותו שבוע היתה התוכניה מונחת על השולחן והילדים היו
מעיינים בה ואף מראים אותה, על תמונותיה, לחבריהם,
בצירוף דברי הסברה. באחת הפעמים הללו פנה אבנר לפתע
אל אמו ובקולו טרוניה:

— אבל, אמא, את העיקר לא סיפרת לנו מה בעצם
פירוש השם "ענבל"?

— "ענבל" — היא לשון הפעמון! הלשון המקשקשת
ומשמיעה את הצליל!

— הם רוצים להגיד שהם משמיעים שירים יפים ומראים
ריקודים מעניינים? — ניסה אבנר לפרש.

— ואני חושבת — התערבה סמדר — מפני שהפעמון
המצלצל זהו סמל הצאן המקפצות או הגמל המתנוענע וזהו
חלק מ... המזרח... מן הנוף... ואולי — התעוררה פתאום
— אולי כמו שאבנרי אמר, רק קצת אחרת — שהם משמיעים
צליל חדש, צליל של תימן והווי הארץ ביחד?

— את זאת — אמרה האם כשהיא קמה ופונה למלאכתה,
— את זאת אני משאירה לכם, ילדים, להתווכח, לחשוב ולפרש
בעצמכם, עד — — —

— עד? — שאלו שני הילדים בסקרנות.

— עד ההאזנה־המשותפת הבאה לצלילי ה"ענבל"!

להקת "ענבל" בהוליווד

רקדני ענבל במסיבה החגיגית, בה נפגשו עם כוכבים רבים. בתמונה הם נראים עם הכוכב רוברט ריאן (יושב, במרכז).

בימים אלה הגיע לאימפרסריו י־ אר ולין מכתב מיצחק חבר ל־ הקת "ענבל" המתאר את סיור ח־ הלהקה בארה"ב ובעיקר את בי־ קורה בהוליווד. יצחק, המנגן על הצ'אד הינו _תגלית_ של יאיר ז־ רין ונגינתו המבדיחה את הלהקה משאירה רושם רב על הצופים בהופעה.
חרי לסמוכים מסתכבו בצירוף ב־ מה _תמונות_, עם כוכבים נודעים

מדביק לפני בעת ההופעה, ובחוץ איני נוקק לקיושוטים מיוחדים לפני. כן נם־ גשתי עם האמרגן סול יורוק, ששאל עלי פרטים רבים.
אחרי כן הסתובבתי בהוליבוד — די התאכזבתי. חשבתי שמי יודע מה אראה כאן — ובסוף זו עיר רגילה. בכל זאת, ראיתי את התיאטרון הסיני, שם מוטבֵ־ עים כפות ידיהם ורגליהם של כל הכו־ כבים הגדולים על המדרכה. ואחר בקרנו במצפה הכוכבים שנראה בסרט "מרד הנ־ עורים" — ממנו אפשר לראות את כל לוס אנג'לס. ומכאן זה באמת מראה מר־ היב.
בקרנו גם בבית הקברות ההוליבודי. ראינו קברותיהם של כוכבים — בינינו של ט'רון פאור ושל רודולף ולנ־ טינו. הוא מת לפני קלוסים שנה, ומאז יום מותו באה אשה, לא_נשה שחורים, יום יום אל הקבר, ומניחה עליו זר פרחים רענן!

*

לפני שבועיים בקרנו באולפני "פרי מונט". ראינו את הבימות השונות ואת ניר לואיס בזמן הסרטת סרטו החדש. ניר זה — מוקוין בחסד, התפעלצנו מצ־ חוק כשראינו אותו. אחרי שסים, הצט־ למנו אתו — ותואר לך את הפתחעבה כ־ שאמר, בעברית: "ברוך אתה ה' אלֵ־ הינו מלך העולם, אשר בחר בנו מכל העמים..." על הבימה ראינו גם את מורים שבלייה. שהוא אדם מקסים. ניר לואיס, אגב, הזמין אותנו לארוחת צהרים. אחרי כן בקרנו באולפני יוניברסל, שם ראינו את בינג קלי ואת ספנסר טריייסי בעבו־ דתם. לא יכולנו להצטלם עמם, כיון שע־ סרקום היו בעבודתם משך שעות רבות, ולא יכלו להתפנות.
אחרי הופעה ניסמת, שהצליחה, אף היא

בהופעה הראשונה שלנו, שהתקיימה במ־ לון "ריץ", נכחו אישים רבים ובניהם שחקני קולנוע רבים — טוני קרטיס ד־ ג'נט ליי, אסתר וויליאמס שבאה עם ג'ף צ'אנדלר, דינה שור ורוברט מונטגומרי והספנטומאי מרסל מרסו. האורֵירה היתה חגיגית — בחוף היו זרקורי ענק, כש־ מרות שוטרים והמולה רבה.
ההופעה הצליחה היטב, והצטלמנו עם הכוכבים שבאו לראותנו. באותו ערב נ־ ערכה לכבודנו מסיבה במלון הענק בבר־

במסיבה אחרת נפגשו רקדני הלהקה עם אסתר וויליאמס, שהזמינה אותם למסיבה משלה — ואף רקדה עמם ריקוד הורה מחבר

The Inbal dance company in the newspapers

The Decline of Inbal

In the early years Sara Levy-Tanai insisted that the Inbal dancers only be of Yemenite descent, as she needed those sources to inspire the works of choreography she created and processed. As long as the human roster was entirely Yemenite Sara Levy could continue creating her works to great success. As the years passed, dancers slowly began drifting away, replaced by others of non-Yemenite descent who were far from Yemenite tradition. It was strange to see these dancers in folklore performances such as "A Wedding in Yemen" and other pieces. Despite the Yemenite costumes, the dancers could not blur their identities with their movements.

When the sources of inspiration Sara was tapping dried up and vanished, she was forced to consider creative ideas that did not require a particular cultural background. What was important to her at this point was that the new dancers at least had the technical ability to adapt themselves to the Inbal style of movement. But as time passed it was clear that Sara could not reach the same level of success with her new dancers as she had with her first group. This had a considerable influence on her new works, and her last pieces did not achieve the same level of success.

This became apparent in the dance company's artistic and financial state, and in the audience that stayed away from her shows. This continued for a few years until at a meeting of the Inbal Public Council it was decided to replace Sara Levy-Tanai.

Like many of Inbal's supporters, it was hard for me to process the overthrow of Sara Levy-Tanai, a founder of theater and recipient of the Israel Prize.

But there was nothing to be done about it, the Council opened a legal bid to choose a dance company director and, among others, approached me. I came in for an interview, equipped with two programs for work with the dance company, and I was asked several questions, including how much time I would need to get the dance company back on its feet. I told them it would take eight months to a year, and then they told me that **Moshe Efrati**, director of the "Sound and Silence" dance company, said it would take at least three years, and asked how I could do it in a third of the time. I told them: "Gentlemen, I used to be part of Inbal, I watched their shows, I know their problems and everything they need.

I know the language of Inbal." They heard me, thanked me, and that was the end of it.

Some time later I learned that **Margalit Oved**, among the first dancers the band had ever had, who at the time was working in California, was chosen for the role. Of course, I later learned that the bid was rigged in advance.

I was present at the theater for Margalit Oved's premiere. The Public Council was there as well. During the intermission one of the Council members approached and said he was sorry I hadn't been selected.

Since then the Inbal dance company has been unable to recreate its glory days, and its success has declined and withered away over the years.

Despite my respect and love for Sara Levy-Tanai, I disagreed with her on quite a few subjects. Among other things, she did nothing to cultivate young talent among the Inbal dancers who could, in time, continue the dance company's traditions. She didn't believe and had no faith in any of her dancers. To her, the present was more important than the future, and her lack of encouragement and respect for her students buried any possibility of a second generation. More than once, in moments of frustration, we dared tell Sara that after she died her tombstone would read: "After my death I don't care if the sun never shines again." Sara Levy-Tanai heard our words but chose to ignore them.

The HaPa'amonim Dance Company

After touring with Inbal in America, I decided to start my own dance company. It was 1962 and my partners in founding the dance company were **Yona Levy**, a graduate of Mia Arbatova's school and a main dancer at Inbal, and her husband **Yitzchak Eliezerov**, the musician and chang player. Within six months the HaPa'amonim dance company was up on its feet and started performing on behalf of the government's Tourism Bureau before groups of tourists from all over the world. HaPa'amonim's success was beyond all expectations. In the first phase we had a program that lasted 45 minutes, and over time I added another 45 minutes. With a program lasting an hour and a half I believed it was best to rent the Mugrabi Theater in order to appear before a wide audience.

Yona Levy and me performing "Bukhari Wedding"

The first performance opened with a press conference presenting the dance company to the media. The show included a modern take on an Israeli medley, folklore segments – Yemenite dancers (male), a "Chabani Dance" by Yona Levy and me, "Original Arabic Debka", "Bukhari Wedding" with the help and assistance of **Menachem and Bracha Eliezerov**, z"l, the parents of Yitzchak Eliezerov, who were artists at heart in the fullest sense of the term – and for the finale we performed shepherd's dances and shepherd's games. I invited Sara Levy-Tanai to this performance, along with my friends from Inbal. The next day I bought all the newspapers featuring reviews of the show. To my surprise all the reviews were positive, without exception, and this became the topic of conversation for the day. The Inbal dancers were curious to hear what Sara thought of the show. Her response was that the success of my choreography was a complete coincidence and nothing more than a passing fad.

Bracha and Menachem Eliezerov, z"l

Some time later, in 1963, the Ministry of Foreign Relations approached Inbal with an offer to perform in an Israeli pavilion at the international expo in Canada, but when the delegation began its preparations it became clear there would only be room for half the Inbal members at the pavilion. Sara was unwilling to split the dance company and was asked whether she could recommend another dance company whose size met the requirements of the Israeli pavilion. Sara Levy-Tanai recommended HaPa'amonim and invited me to a conversation at the Inbal studio. After explaining the situation, she made it clear that while she had recommended my dance company, she did not consider HaPa'amonim actual competition to Inbal. I told Sara that she had nothing to fear, though I privately thought the fact that Sara mentioned Inbal and HaPa'amonim in the same breath was in itself a compliment to me. Sara also added that no other dance company in Israel could match Inbal. Of course, I politely affirmed her words. Unfortunately, the trip to Canada on behalf of the Ministry of Foreign affairs ultimately did not come to pass.

Yona Levy and me performing "Chabani Dance"

The HaPa'amonim dance company performing "Bukhari Wedding"

The HaPa'amonim dancers in a Yemenite medley

Bukhari Wedding

The HaPa'amonim dancers in an Arabic debka

HaPa'amonim in "Bukhari Wedding"

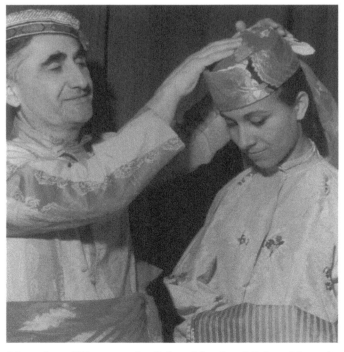

Menachem Eliezerov, the father, blessing Miriam Menashe

The HaPa'amonim dance company in shepherd's dances and games, in Paris, France

HaPa'amonim performing at the Estoril Casino in Portugal

HaPa'amonim performing at the Estoril Casino in Portugal

Debka Uriya

A Yemenite dance in Kfar HaMaccabia

From the Yemenite medley

HaPa'amonim on Dutch television

Singer Aharon Amram, the anthologist of Yemenite song

Dancers in Yemenite clothes

Visitors from America at HaPa'amonim's rehearsal house

A group from HaPa'amonim flying to London for a television appearance

HaPa'amonim performing

לפני הקלעים

„פעמונים"

(להקה ישראלית לפולקלור, מחול וזמר)

היה זה ערב תיאטרון חם באולם מוגרבי.

אך הקהל הרגיש את עצמו נפלא. אולם התיאטרון הישן כאילו נעשה חדש וצעיר יותר. גערות ונערות צעירים עד מאד ורחימניים עד־מאד ישבו על הבמה ומילאו את האולם מפה אל פה. ממש קירבות גלויות היא מקהלה זו. אם כי חבריה ברובם בני העדה התימנית הם, משתתפים בה גם יוצאי בוכארה ו„אשכנזים"...

הדברים שמעלים אמנים צעירים אלה על קרשי הבמה, קרוב הוא מאד לליבו של הקהל הישראלי האמיתי. יש כאן ריח וטעם מיוחד, זה הוא המדבר יש תב־ ליני ערב, ועל הבמה מופיע גוף המוצא של עמנו...

בעולם מושחת זה של מיניות גסה וח־ סרת־בושה בתקופת ה„סטריפ־טיז" וה־ „טוויסט" מהווים מחולות להקה זו נווה מדבר ירוק של אהבה אנושית אמיתית. הרגישות הבאים לידי ביטוי בריקוד זה, ובשירה זו, מתעלים כאן כבאורח־פלא אל ספירות הרוח, ופונים לצד הטוב ש־ בנפש האדם.

המרכז הנראה בהצגה היא הכרקדנית יונה לוי־אליעזרוב, זה־מכבר רקדנית זו את לב הקהל הישראלי. וזה בשל נאמנותה לאמנותה לארצה. והרי עמדה יונה לוי־אליעזרוב כבר באור הזר קורים, שיחקה בסרט — „מארקו פולו" — ומצאה די־כוח בנפשה לשוב אל הארץ אליה היא שייכת, ואמנם המעשה שהיא עושה עתה שירות הוא, שירות לאומי ותרבותי כאחת.

היא מחוללת בטכניקה מושלמת. לפר־ קים יש בריקודיה אף משום וירטואו־ זיות, אך השכלול הטכני אינו פוגם כחן הטבעי שלה ובתום הנעורים של אמנותה. כל ה„מספרים" שבהופעת המקהלה עו־ לים יפה ואחדים מהם אף מזהירים. ואפילו טובים מאד לפי קנה־מידה עולמי. כך למשל דומה ה„תתונה הבוכארית" למ־ כך נדיר מארץ זו או לגובלין בצבעים וצורות־היפים ביותר.

משה יצחק הלוי הוא בן זוג, היאה ליונה לוי, וזהו אמן עצמאי בעל יכולת טכנית רבה ובעל לב ונפש. הוא מנהלה האמנותי של המקהלה והכוריאוגראף.

*

ישנם בהצגה אף גיבורים בלתי־נראים לעיין: עוזרו של המנהל, יצחק אליעז־ רוב, אמנון מגורו כהן, התמאורן המצו־ יין, וכל להקה־כולה המצטיינת במש־ חקה המתואם והההרמוני.

יוסף רפאל

מסך ומסבה

יונה לוי אליעזרוב ומשה יצחק הלוי בריקוד החבאני

להקת „הפעמונים" בטלביזיה האנגלית

[article text columns]

Positive reviews of HaPa'amonim in Israeli newspapers

להקה ישראלית לפולקלור

במה למחול וזמר

משה יצחק הלוי

משה יצחק הלוי (30), הנראה צעיר הרבה משנותיו,
נתקל בעולם הקסם של המחול בגיל מאוחר יחסית.

משה יצחק הלוי, צבר, ממשפחה תימנית ותיקה בארץ –
התגלה על-ידי מיא ארבטובה. בן 17 הוא כבר מופיע
בלהקתה. שפת התנועות כבשה את לבו בסערה והוא מחליט
להקדיש את עצמו למחול. שנה לאחר מכן הוא מתגייס לצה"ל
ומופיע בלהקת הכרמל.

לאחר השחרור, הוא מופיע ב"לי-לה-לו" ונמנה עם
ראשוני המצטרפים ל"דו-רה-מי" של ג'ורג' ואל המנוח.
הוא מתבלט בהצגות "שלום-שלום", "בתיאבון, ישראל!", "חופשה בוונציה"
ו"משחקי הפיז'מה".

אך עולם האופרטה אינו מספק אותו. להקת הבלט המודרני של נעמי
אלסקובסקי היא התחנה הבאה בדרכו, לפני יציאתו עם להקת "ענבל" לסיורה
הכפול בארה"ב ואירופה. הוא יוצר את ריקודיו הראשונים: דבקה אוריה,
דבקה כנען, "עת דודים כלה" ודבקה כורדית. ריקודיו מתחבבים במהירות
ונפוצים בחוגי רקודי עם בארץ. הוא מוזמן ע"י תרצה הודס להדריך את חוגי
הריקוד של ההסתדרות, מדריך את להקת הריקודים של הסטודנטים הירושלמים
היוצאים לסייר בחו"ל ואת להקת הסטודנטים של הטכניון במסעה לאירופה.

הוא מוזמן להדריך את להקת הריקודים היוצאת לפסטיבאל וינה,
ומחוללותיו מקבלים מדליית כסף.

From HaPa'amonim's program

From HaPa'amonim's program. Yona Levy and me in Chabani Dance

ו החדשות

המתרחש בעולם הבד — סרטים, תפקידים ומאורעות אישיים

תמונה ראשונה של יונה מ„מרקו פולו"

ד'ש לקוראי „עולם הקולנע"

ביום ה' שעבר הגיע יצחק אליעזרוב לבלגרד, הצטרף לרעייתו יונה — שאותו יום עצמו החלה בהצלומים הי ממשיים ל„מרקו פולו" לי אחר שער אז עסקי כהכנות וכהצטלומי מבחן. כותב לנו יצחק, מבלגרד :

...הגעתי לבלגרד ביום בו התחלה ההסרטה הממשית. לאחר שהגעתי לבית המלון, נסעתי מיד — בחברת משה יצחק חלוי — לבימת ההסרטה הענקית, ר זאת — במכונית מיוחדת. עליה היה שלט גדול : „מרקו פולו". שם פגשתי לראשונה את יונה, לבושה בבגדי נסיכה, לצורך תפ־ קידה בסרט — ואתם יכולים לת־ אר לעצמכם איזו פגישה נרגשת התחוללה בינינו...

„כעבור דקות מספר החלו ב־ הסרטה, בתוך תפאורה נהדרת של ארמון מלכותי — כשהמוני פ־ רו/קסטורים מסביב. על שני בס־ אות מלכותיים ישבו יונה ודר רותי נגדירג', המגלמת את דמות ודרתה. הקטע המצולם היה מש־ חק השוה בין אלן דילון לבין בן הסולטן — כשלסלי התנאים המוק־ דמים המנצח זוכה בנסיכה אד־ אנה (יונה) והמפסיד — ראשו נכרת. היה מעניין ביותר לחזות בהסרטה.

...זוהי לויהרלוהרזהריב. בתמונה ראשונה מתוך „מרקו פולו".

Yona Levy was invited to star in the film Marco Polo

Dance company Director of Inbal

In 1971, after ten years of independent work, I was once again asked to return to Inbal, this time as dance company director. I accepted the position, though it exceeded its own definition by including technique classes for dancers, planning the work week, managing rehearsals and performing as a dancer, flutist and drummer. One day I was called in for a difficult conversation with Sara Levy-Tanai regarding the work schedule I'd set up. She didn't like it, as I'd changed the order of lessons – I had put a class by **Rina Sharet** first and followed it by Sara Levy-Tanai's. When she asked why I had done so, I explained to her that it was at the dancers' request, claiming that it was hard for them to go from working intensely and exhaustively with Sara to working with Rina Sharet, who was calmer. Rina came to rehearsals better prepared in terms of choreography. Sara disagreed and felt it was a stinging blow to her position and prestige.

One day as we were discussing choreography and choreographers, Sara said that if she ever allowed anyone else to choreograph Inbal, it would be people like **Anna Sokolow**, Jerome Robbins and **Ram-Gopal (the Indian)**, it never even occurred to her that someone among the Inbal dancers might be able to choreograph. I had done so before, even composing two choreographed works – an original Yemenite dance for men and a Chabani dance for the program consisting of short parts called Miniatures, but this had been allowed due to certain circumstances and not Sara's good intentions. After me came **Shlomo Haziz**, z"l, with a choreographed piece called "The Baton". Later came **Leah Avraham, Ilana, Malka, Racheli, Sara'le**, but all these had to fight for it, each with their own story of struggle.

In the twilight of Sara Levy-Tanai's reign as director of Inbal, I came to see the dance company's new program. With me were a couple of my friends, Shefi and Yael – Israelis staying in Melbourne and working in the field of Israeli folk dances. I introduced Sara to my friends and told her that they had donated to Inbal, at my recommendation, a sum of four thousand dollars (!). During the introductory conversation my friend asked Sara why she did not use my talents and skills for Inbal's purposes. Sara's answer was half-serious, half-joking: "Moshiko's career is already over." I was not surprised; I knew to expect no other reaction from her.

But despite our disagreements and misunderstandings, my work at Inbal with

Sara Levy-Tanai aided me greatly in making my own way in the field of dance. I learned a lot from Sara's struggle and the road to fulfilling her dream. Through her, and thanks to Inbal, I achieved things I continue to implement in my work to this day.

Gurit Kadman – A Prophet of Her Generation

Gurit Kadman was a known personality to anyone who dealt with folklore in general and folk dancing in particular. She had dedicated all her time and energy to advancing and developing Israeli folk dancing. As a prophet of her generation and with an uncompromising vision she led the cause of dancers.

Gurit was involved in all dance activities in Israel, from large festivals to personal visits with dance groups in the Jewish, Arab, Druze and Circassians villages and settlements. She encouraged the establishment of ethnic dance groups in most settlements in Israel and enriched us with sources and roots we didn't know we had.

Her vision compelled Gurit to find a common denominator among the different pieces of respective folklore, by turning them into one body that would integrate itself into Israeli culture. Using her own funds, she photographed and documented dance groups that had made their first steps in Israel. She understood this had to be done soon, before time would blur and erase their unique features. Gurit spent days and nights on her sacred work, no one could stop her. To me Gurit Kadman was an admirable figure. Her decency and integrity served as an example to anyone who knew her.

In 1959 I used my night off from Inbal performances and went to a dance night that was held at Beit HaPoel, on Ussishkin Street in Tel-Aviv. The instructor was my friend **Danny Uziel**, one of the HaPoel Tel-Aviv dancers who was pleased to see me. I sat by the stage and followed the dancers, but it was hard for me to enjoy the foreign music and the folk dances performed to its melodies, such as "Krakoviak", "Cherkessia" and "Polka".

At the end of the evening, Danny asked me for my impressions. I did not respond. He understood that I'd been disappointed and said: "Maybe you should do something?" I told him: "No way, I've never put so much as two steps together. But if this is what our dances look like today, how will they look in five years?"

And to myself I thought the state of folk dancing had to improve, and I couldn't wait for time to do its work. That night the subject kept me awake. I had trouble sleeping.

From Spontaneous Improvisation to "Debka Uriya"

One day, when I was still a dancer for Inbal, Sara Levy-Tanai invited Gurit Kadman to one of the rehearsals to lecture us on folk dancing, ethnic dances and ritualistic dances in Israel and the Mediterranean. I was charmed and hypnotized. Gurit's fascinating words sparked my imagination. Different movements began to run through my mind, and made me want to get up, leap to the stage and begin dancing. And so it was. At the end of the lecture I jumped onto the stage and started making unconscious movements. This lasted for a few minutes until I "awoke" to the sound of applause from my friends who'd been watching. They began flooding me with different questions – where did those special moves I'd made come from, what was the dance I'd danced? I couldn't reply, I myself hadn't yet processed what I'd done. Subconsciously I understood that I'd improvised something, but I couldn't quite define it yet.

In all the years of my career I never dared improvise, since I got lucky and never had to audition in an artistic framework. If my fate had been different, I might not be writing these lines now…

For a week I managed to recreate one step after another, until it was clear I'd assembled six sections with each being different from its predecessor.

Since there was no tune to accompany my first dance, I decided to base it on a drumbeat alone. Later I came to learn an anonymous tune played by Tzefion Atzata (Chotem), z"l (mentioned previously). Over time I learned that the tune, which was still nameless, had been composed by **Nechamia Sharabi**, brother of the singer **Boaz Sharabi**. The music matched the rhythm and structure of the dance I'd composed, as though it had been composed specifically for that purpose. I gave the dance the name "Debka Uriya", after my eldest son who had at the time just turned two. I decided to give him my first creation as a birthday present.

The person who spread word of Debka Uriya was a dancer in Inbal named **Nechamia Cohen**. Within days I received an invitation from Aya, the dance company coordinator for the Kibbutzim movement, from Ein Harod, to come and teach the dance company Debka Uriya.

The Dance Festival in Vienna

In 1959 the Kibbutzim dance company set out for a dance festival in Vienna, in which dance companies from every socialist country in the world were participating. The dance company convened for a month of rehearsals at the Shfayim kibbutz. Day after day, upon completing my work with Inbal, I would go to Shfayim to work with the Kibbutzim dance company on the Debka Uriya choreography. Rehearsals began at three in the afternoon and ended at ten at night. Despite my minimal experience in the field of choreography I managed to put a different and stylistically unique folklore experience on the stage.

After the month of rehearsals, the dance company performed at the kibbutz amphitheater as a gesture to the farmers and to important guests for hosting the dance company there, as well as building the show's program. My teacher Mia Arbatova and Sara Levy-Tanai were on the panel of judges. The dance company's repertoire was based on an old medley from previous programs. Debka Uriya was the only new dance. As it approached the host took the stage and named me as the choreographer of the choreography. I wasn't sitting in the audience, I was too excited and preferred to stand behind the scenes, next to the stage. I watched the crowd welcome the men of the dance company who danced Debka Uriya with thunderous applause, even compelling them to come back for an encore.

That night I felt I'd earned great success and received good reviews from Mia Arbatov and Sara Levy-Tanai. However, Nechamia Sharabi, the choreographer of the music for the dance who was also present that evening, approached me at the end of the show and expressed his disappointment and anger for the host failing to credit him as the musical choreographer. I tried to explain that I hadn't known in advance what the host would or would not say. I told him we were both just starting out and our future lay ahead of us, and we should know how to deal with situations like this, but Nechamia Sharabi stood his ground. In protest he decided to write lyrics for the melody and call the song "Debka HaAbir (Debka Habir)". At that point our paths separated.

Baptism of Fire

At the dance festival in Vienna I was told that the men of the Kibbutzim dance company had won second place in the men's dancing competition, with my Debka Uriya, and returned with a silver medal. First place went to the Yugoslavian dance company, and third place to the Russians. Following that success, I received an invitation from the "Department of Folk Dances", managed by **Tirtza Hodes**, to attend workshops where I could teach my dance. I tried to explain to Tirtza that due to its nature and technical requirements, Debka Uriya was a stage piece and not a folk dance. Tirtza claimed that the demand to learn the dance came from the instructors and dancers and asked me to consider their request.

I suggested teaching other dances I'd managed to compose since Debka Uriya, like Et Dodim Kala, Debka Knaan and Debka Kurdit, but I was refused. After considering the matter, I decided to accept the offer.

I arrived at the Histadrut Activists' House, which was swarming with participants. Dance choreographers were there, and of course the folk dancing elite such as Gurit Kadman, Tirtza Hodes, **Shalom Hermon, Rivka Sturman, Leah Bergstein** and others.

The time came for me to teach. I was introduced for the first time to the crowd of dancers, some of whom knew me from my time as an Inbal dancer. The noise was deafening, and it was hard for me to teach the class. I asked for quiet again and again, but no one paid attention to my request. I couldn't accept the participants' lack of discipline. At some point I lost my temper and yelled at them: "Anyone who wants to talk, get out!" For a moment silence reigned in the theater. It was perhaps the first time anyone had ever shouted at them so aggressively.

After my lesson I was approached by Shalom Hermon, z"l, among the founders of Israeli folk dancing, a man of noble heart and an educator. He put his hand on my shoulder and tried to calm me down. "You have to understand that what happens here is a social event, it's natural to have a little loud excitement," he said. It was a nice gesture on his part. I explained my position and added that I didn't know if I wanted to continue in this field, but if I did, I would prefer to be known as someone who took his work seriously and did not put up with inappropriate behavior, even if it's just folk dancing. Ultimately, I passed my first baptism by fire successfully, and subsequently there were many invitations to teach my new dances, whether in workshops or at the instructors' training ulpanim.

Fearless and Without Bias

An extraordinary event happened during one of the workshops I was attending. Rivka Sturman, z"l, who was considered one of the most well-known creators and pioneers of folk dancing in the country, had just finished teaching her dance, the name of which I cannot recall. The dancers were concerned about the quality of that dance. Gurit Kadman was also disappointed. She took the small stage in the theater, and used the microphone to address Rivka, asking her with extremely harsh words to stop bringing those types of dances. That's how Gurit was, a fearless woman without bias who always got to the point, and never hesitated to cut the small talk.

The Instructors' Training Ulpanim

Even at the start of my journey, with the success of my first dances like Debka Uriya, Debka Knaan, Debka Kurdit and Et Dodim Kala, I was asked by the Department of Folk Dances to teach my dances at the instructors' training ulpans, which were scattered throughout the country from north to south. I accepted the task, as it was important to my personal development and to the strengthening of my relationship with the student public in the ulpan. And it was indeed an unforgettable experience. For the first time the students were exposed to my style of dance and a method of instruction they were not familiar with. The trainees' personal skill levels, usually low-to-medium, made it difficult for them to deal with my dances, which were elaborate and based on ethnic elements which were uncommon in the terminology in Israeli folk dancing, requiring a certain level of technique.

From the start it was clear there wasn't much I could change in a single meeting, yet I tried to cultivate their belief that they were capable of more. It was important to me that they understood and internalized the meaning and responsibility of being certified folk dancing instructors.

When the ulpanim first began, the Department of Folk Dances emphasized the personality of the student – the future instructor – and subsidized part of their annual tuition. At first it was determined that the instructor training ulpan would take three years. The second ulpan was cut to two years, and as time passed it was cut again to just one year. How much material could you squeeze into one meeting a week, for just one year, with so many disruptive holidays, unless you were lucky enough to be dealing with savants?

The more I met with the ulpan students, the more I was convinced that the lesson plan had to be changed, to prioritize more important areas pertaining to molding the future instructor's personality, and improve their technical capabilities so they would know how to cope with complex movements. I spoke with the Department of Folk Dances, which was responsible for the ulpanim, and told them they had to challenge the students. I noted that it was important the ulpan be granted a more serious image and perhaps even academic standing. A certificate alone did not promise success. An instructor who lacked charisma and whose personality did not radiate onto their students would not last very long.

Unfortunately, my impression was that the supervisors were content with the status quo. I heard more than once from students that the ulpan was not challenging enough for them, even bored them, and all that mattered was getting the certificate at the end of the year. This concerned me deeply, especially when I recalled Gurit Kadman who always hoped to see the ulpan alumni go out into the field, to document material that might someday be enriched and diversified. I was sorry to see her dream fade away.

These days there are several ulpanim for training instructors – one in Jerusalem, run by **Azariela and Yael Yaacobi**, and the other at Tel-Aviv University, managed by **Gadi Bitton**. I have the impression that the ulpanim continue with the basic format of their predecessors. I hope I'm wrong about that. As for the certificate, I humbly believe only the ones who were "chosen by the profession" will succeed.

Tirtza Hodes – Director of the Department of Folk Dances

In mid-1960 HaPa'amonim performed throughout Israel. As the dance company's director and choreographer, I dedicated two hours a day to sitting at Café Noga, on the corner of Pinsker and Mugrabi Square in Tel-Aviv. Every day in the afternoon the café served as a center and meeting place for artists. Personal phones weren't commonplace yet and Café Noga's phone served as the main channel of communications between the artistic elements in the country.

It was used to order performances and finalize collaborations.

One day a call was made to the café. I was called to the phone. On the other end of the line was Tirtza Hodes, director of the Department of Folk Dances in the HaPoel Committee of the Histadrut (as mentioned previously). Tirtza sounded excited and said: "Moshiko, don't move, an official car is coming your way with two men from Persia (Iran), guests of the Ministry of Foreign Affairs. They'll take you with them to the Afula ulpan for training." "But I don't have an ulpan in Afula today," I wondered. Tirtza explained that the trip had been specially organized so the Persian guests could see me in action.

I told her I had to run home and get my bag with the instructing equipment – flutes, gym shoes and appropriate clothing – before I went on my way. By the time I made it back to Café Noga the official car was already waiting for me. I went inside, shook hands with the guests and during our ride it became clear that one of them managed the Museum of Folklore in Persia, while the other was related to the Shah's family. Israel was their last stop on a tour of several countries in Eastern Europe, seeking a choreographer for some work in Persia. They explained that an Eastern European candidate was unacceptable to them, due to the obvious Russian influence on the region's artistic style, so they preferred to find the right person in Israel, in light of the friendly relations between Persia and Israel during the Shah's reign.

On the way back from Afula one of them told me: "You know our country is very wealthy. If you come to us we'll compensate you appropriately." And before we parted ways he said: "You'll be hearing from us." I was thrilled, and eagerly awaited their invitation.

Weeks passed, but nothing happened. One day Gurit Kadman met me and asked: "Have you packed your suitcase yet?" "No, they haven't gotten back to me yet," I said, still hoping.

Two or three months later it turned out that **Rina Sharet**, a dance teacher and folklore instructor, had been chosen to go to Persia. I suppose that's what the Ministry of Foreign Affairs preferred.

Some years passed, and Rina Sharet published her new book "My Fate Comes Calling". In one chapter she told the story of her trip to Persia and her work there. It turned out that in fact three people had been candidates for this trip: **Yonatan Karmon**, who was certainly the first person Tirtza approached, had refused. She apparently turned to me afterwards, without mentioning other candidates, and Rina Sharet was the third. Unfortunately, to this day I don't know who meddled in whose affairs, but Gurit Kadman expressed to me her disappointment that I hadn't been chosen to go to Persia.

Working with Minority Dance Companies

In 1966 the Arab department of the General Histadrut invited me to serve as artistic director, instructor and choreographer for minority dance companies – Cherkasies, Druze and Arabs. I had always been interested in these ethnic groups, and this request gave me the perfect opportunity to get to know them up close. I was happy to accept the position.

First, I wanted to learn about the traditions and the cache of elemental movements they used; only then did I translate all this information into choreography requirements.

The problem with all three dance companies was that the movement set on which they based their dances was too limited. I wanted to help encourage them to develop additional elements. I intended to build more than one choreography set for each dance company so as not to lose the authenticity of their movements on the stage, in the absence of their natural environment.

The Kfar-Kama Circassians dance company I instructed

My first meeting was with the Circassians dance company from Kfar-Kama. I arrived at the village with **Victor Sharabani**, the cultural representative appointed on behalf of the Arab department of the General Histadrut. We met the village secretary, who laid out the dance company's problems and difficulties before us, and then we turned to the village's cultural hall where the dance company was waiting for us. The hall was packed from end to end.

The villagers were curious to see their dance company's new Israeli instructor. We were forced to carve a path through the crowd to the front row, where seats had been reserved for us. Mr. Sharabani introduced me to the dancers. After our introduction I asked the dance company to demonstrate some of their dances for me. Accompanied by an accordionist, they danced for barely ten minutes, or to be more precise they improvised with no organization. They called the first demonstration "Cherkasia" and the second "Sesan". They were based on elements drawn from Circassians tribal dances. After the performance I spoke with the Circassians dance company members and explained to them that we had a lot of work ahead of us. From our first meeting it was clear to me that the young dance company members knew very little about Circassians dance tradition, which forced me to create ex nihilo. From one rehearsal to the next we progressed, and in a short time we managed to make "Cherkasia" and "Sesan" two complete and harmonious works of choreography. When my work with the Cherkasies became routine, the women of the village began sewing costumes for the dance company.

Me with the Circassians dance company

My next meeting was with the Druze dance company from the village of Osafiya on Mount Carmel. The dance company was comprised of young dancers from the "Working and Learning Youth" group in the village. My visit to Osafiya was similarly greeted with great excitement on the part of the villagers. They crowded the windows of the hall, which was in fact a small chamber. Victor Sharabani and I sat in the corner of the room while the dance company stood on the opposite corner and prepared the first demonstration.

Me with the Druze dance company from the village of Osafiya in the Carmel

The flutist began to play, and the dance company danced, but they were disorganized and there was no connection between the dancers and the music. I had to interrupt the "dance" in order to make my comments, but the dance company instructor **Munir** was upset by my words. I asked the dance company to repeat the part. During the second demonstration there was once again an incompatibility between the flutist and the dancers. Again, I had to ask the dance company to stop the dance. This time I approached the flutist and explained that he had to adjust himself to the rhythm of the dance. Munir was furious and said playing the flute was harder than playing the accordion. The atmosphere in the hall was tense. I decided to take a surprising step to restore the trust between us. I asked for the flutist's instrument and for the band to stand in the corner and prepare to start the dance again. I brought the flute to my lips and played the notes that were familiar to the dancers. The dancers "turned to stone" and couldn't take the first step. Munir was confused as well. He immediately went to Victor Sharabani and asked him if I was really an Israeli Jew or an Arab. He said he had never met an Israeli Jew who could play the "Shbaba" (Arab flute) that way. We set things straight and all parted ways eager for the next meeting.

The third dance company was the Arab band from the village of Tira. Every time I arrived in one of the villages the village boys would wait for me at the entrance, escort me to the rehearsal hall and watch the Israeli dance their dances and play their melodies on their flutes.

I have no doubt that my work with these dance companies made it possible for me to study the roots of their culture in music and dance up close. This aided me in constructing choreography for their dances and preparing them for future performances.

Then the stage of costumes arrived. The Druze and Arabs asked to wear Israeli-style outfits, but I convinced them to take pride in their traditional garb and wear them to their dances.

After a year of joint work, the three dance companies were invited to perform for an entire week at the "Mizrachi Market" held at "Kolbo Shalom". The crowd visiting the location was deeply impressed by the performances. For the dancers, it was their first attempt to present their culture to the Israeli public and earn confidence that would accompany them into the future.

The Circassians dance company performing

After four years of working with the minority dance companies, I received a request from the managers of the Leiden City Festival in Holland to participate in the festival. I took the Circassians and Druze dance companies with me and added a Yemenite group. From Holland we continued on to another festival in the city of Schoten in Belgium. Both festivals saw the mixed group of dancers achieve great success.

My work with these dance companies greatly contributed to and influenced the dances I composed for Israeli folk dancing. Many of the debka-style dances flourished thanks to this influence. For five years we worked together, and I felt that as much as I contributed to the Circassians, Druze and Arab dance companies, they had given and enriched me much more.

A Fateful Turn

In 1968 the three minority dance companies were invited to participate in the Dalia Festival, held at Kibbutz Dalia. It was meant to be my last activity in the field of Israeli folk dancing. The Department of Folk Dances promised to look into opportunities for me to work with Yemenite groups as well. I waited for the Department's response, but it never came. Finally, **Bentzi Tiram**, z"l, got the job with the Yemenites, without any explanation offered to me.

When I arrived at the festival campgrounds for final rehearsals, I had already made the decision to end my career in the field of Israeli folk dances, after nine difficult years which first seemed glamorous and promising and ended poorly and bitterly. I felt that I was constantly being sabotaged and held back, that my dance style was intimidating, that I was under pressure to give up and quit. It was a chain of events that had been building up for years.

If a drop of water dripping on a concrete floor can eventually wear a hole in it, the same is true of a flesh-and-blood person under various types of pressure, failing to cope because of their dependency on other people around them. If no help is offered, then where is society's responsibility to them; or is it society that creates these pressures in order to drive the individual to a certain conclusion?

A Dutch couple were wandering the festival grounds – a man and woman, representing the Nevo dancer's organization in Holland. They came to watch the festival and, at the same time, meet with me and invite me to Holland to teach my dances at the organization's annual meeting in the city of Arnhem.

I was surprised to be approached. Such a possibility had never occurred to me before, and perhaps I'd been naïve. Regardless, after recovering from the surprise I turned down the Nevo representatives. They were surprised as well and asked why I'd refused. I explained that I had decided to quit folk dancing after the festival. They said they respected my decision but asked me to hold off on my retirement until after my visit to Holland. To persuade me they said that some of my dances were popular and performed in Holland.

An Israeli Folk Dance Workshop in Holland

I asked for a two-day reprieve to consider the matter. I asked myself how I could travel to a foreign country, to people with a different mentality, and bring stylized ethnically influenced dances, while even in Israel dancers found it difficult to cope with my material? It was a difficult deliberation, but I asked myself, what was the worst that could happen? I would go to Holland and have another experience – after all, it was only a four-day workshop, at the end of which I would return home. Two days later the Dutch couple returned to me for their answer. This time I said yes.

The workshop was scheduled for the end of December 1968. At the time I had ten dances under my belt, and I wasn't sure this would be enough. To be sure I decided to take with me the three ethnic dances as well – the Druze, the Circassians and the Arabic Debka – that belonged to the dance companies I'd worked with.

The date of the trip approached; I was thrilled. Even during the flight many thoughts crossed my mind – who would meet me at the airport in Amsterdam? Who would take me to the training camp? What would the accommodations and the food be like? And how would my instruction work as a workshop?

Four hours later the plane landed at the Schiphol airport in Amsterdam, on a snowy runway. A freezing cold ran rampant outside. After passing the routine inspections I left the terminal and headed to my hosts, who were waiting for me. We drove to Arnhem, where the workshop was located.

I was among the first to arrive and had enough time to get organized in my room and rest until the date of the class. I was thrilled and full of anticipation. I cloistered myself in my room and said a little prayer that I would succeed at this task. A knock at the door informed me it was time to go downstairs.

The hall was full, from end to end. Due to its small size the number of participants had been limited to a mere one hundred. I was welcomed with great warmth and thunderous applause. I was stunned. After the excitement died down a bit I began the instruction.

Even with the first dance I was surprised at how quickly the dancers picked up the moves, and how accurate their movements were. Tears of happiness gleamed in my eyes. I couldn't understand how a foreign group so easily and accurately executed my dances, just as I'd seen in my mind's eye. With the end of the session I went up to my room to rest and calm down from the experience, and reconsider my decision to quit folk dancing, after discovering there were those who could indeed cope with my dances both technically and stylistically.

The Dutch dancers were hungry to learn, ready for any technical or stylistic challenge. I also came to learn of their great experience regarding folk dances and folklore. There's a reason the Dutch are considered the best dancers in Europe.

Even before the workshop ended the Nevo representatives approached me and asked if I'd be willing to stay in the area for an additional period to instruct classes in other locations. Without hesitation I agreed, since no work was waiting for me in Israel anyway.

In addition to the regular instruction, I was invited to compose a choreographed piece for one of the popular folklore dance companies in Holland, directed by **Ferdinand**. The choreography was based on Yemenite styles. The dance company used this dance in its repertoire for several years. I also provided special workshops based on the Circassians, Druze and Arabic dances.

My Holland tour lasted for three months and ended with much greater success than I'd anticipated. On my last day, I composed the dance Ki Hivshilu Eshkolot during my lunch break between classes, and taught it accompanied with my flute.

I returned to Israel impressed and full of faith, confidence and a desire to keep creating. My trip to Holland only clarified that I had to stick to my goals and beliefs and continue my work.

Thank you, Dutch dancers, for opening my eyes and helping me see the value of my dances. You restored my confidence and faith in my path, and the desire to continue composing dances. Had it not been for my trip to Holland, I would probably be engaged in a different profession today.

An Instructor on Behalf of the Department of Folk Dances

There is no doubt in my mind that the Department of Folk Dances was a major contributor and positive influence to the direction and development of Israeli folk dancing, its instructors and students. The Department, situated in the HaPoel Committee of the Histadrut, had at the very start of its journey prepared infrastructure which included the workshops, ulpanim for training instructors, dance notes and music, documentary materials, the organization of national festivals, and many more important things.

The status of Tirtza Hodes, a political appointee, was unchallenged. She ran the Department according to her own judgment, and sometimes in opposition to the opinions of activists in the field of folk dance who disagreed with her ways and policies. This caused a rift in the relationship between the two sides, but she made sure to surround herself with those who sided with her and push away her opponents.

In 1972 **Yoav Ashriel**, one of the leading choreographers, decided to cease collaborating with the Department and Tirtza due to a difference of opinion, and hold private workshops which had been the exclusive monopoly of the Department of Folk Dances. Tirtza did not take this kindly and did everything she could to disrupt the classes. She approached creators asking them not to participate, and some dance choreographers acceded to her request and withdrew from participation. Yoav also turned to me asking to take part in his classes. I agreed. When he asked whether I was worried about Tirtza's reaction, I replied that I was no one's property and would not be used as a weapon against someone else.

Of course, I eventually had to pay the price. My participation in Yoav's workshops never came up in conversations between Tirtza and me, but the number of classes I would give on behalf of the Department was cut for some reason, though these were an important source of income for me.

During one conversation I asked Tirtza about the cut in the number of classes. She answered that the ulpan committee had decided to send a creator to each ulpan only once a year. I found that hard to believe and kept asking: "Does that include me and my dances, which ulpan coordinators usually had a difficult time teaching?" Her answer was yes. That's how Tirtza was, and maybe she's best described by the saying: "Your actions will bring you close, and your actions will push you away."

Tirtza had many connections beyond the framework of the Department of Folk Dances, she was also connected with the Department of Foreign Relations, the Ministry of Education and the Jewish Agency, all of whom only bolstered her position. Every dance company heading abroad needed Tirtza's recommendation to receive financial assistance from the government. Anyone wanting to teach at one of the Jewish camps in America, through the Agency, needed her recommendation. Tirtza used her influence on cultural coordinators in Jewish community centers in Germany as well – in Frankfurt and Berlin. Once I was invited by the Cultural Coordinator of the Jewish community in Berlin to prepare a choreographed piece for his dance company's performance. Tirtza found out and made her anger towards that coordinator plain. I don't know why the fact that I'd been invited to Berlin bothered her.

Over the years the Department would hold meetings and supplemental workshops in the summer months as well. Suddenly this activity ceased because Tirtza began traveling to the east coast of the United States on behalf of the Agency to teach Israeli folk dances at a Jewish youth summer camp. Once the camp was over, she could visit her children who were staying in one of the American states and stay there through the end of the summer. Supposedly this need was understandable, but the instructors and dancers thought she was obliged to consider continued summer activity even in her absence. "It's unacceptable," the dancers and instructors said, "that the manager of the Department of Folk Dances will go to America and paralyze the entire Department." But Tirtza ignored the criticism and continued her annual trips to America. This fact caused an uproar among the dancers and instructors, and they were unwilling to accept it. They decided to get organized, set up their own organization and immediately dispose of the services of the Department of Folk Dances.

Establishing a New Organization

In July 1974, ten months after arriving in America, I visited Israel for the first time, for a choreography job with the dance company "Tzavta Yizrael". The dance company was preparing for a tour in America, on behalf of the Israeli manager **Nava Bodinger** who lived in New York. On the first weekend of my stay in Israel I was invited to teach a workshop based on my third published album. The workshop was organized by **Yankale Levy** (Jr.) from Kiryat Bialik's "Beit Katz". During one of the breaks the participants gathered together and presented to me the idea of setting up a new organization. The conversation was electric. Criticisms were made of Tirtza Hodes and the policies of the Department of Folk Dances. I felt the great bitterness of each and every one of the speakers. It wasn't long before the organization was on its feet. Yoav Ashriel, **Tamar Alyagor**, Yankale Levy and more took a considerable part in making the idea a reality. All the creators and instructors joined the new organization, and with its establishment the Department of Folk Dances lost a considerably amount of its power. The new organization was housed in the HaPoel Committee of the Histadrut as well and was recognized as a professional organization in all things.

"Moshiko Festival"

With all the difficulties we'd experienced, whether together or separately, I always believed that my personal relationship with Tirtza Hodes was based on mutual respect and trust. Since I lived in America Tirtza asked that we keep in touch through letters. "It's important for me to hear what you're going through in America," she said. The wish was mutual. It was just as important for me to stay in touch with Tirtza and kept tabs on what was happening in Israel with regards to the field of folk dancing. During my visits to Israel we would meet and talk, each visit included an instruction tour across the country that Tirtza could call the "Moshiko Festival".

Anna Sokolow – A Powerful and Uncompromising Personality

Anna Sokolow, a Jewish-American choreographer with a global reputation, came to Inbal through Jerome Robbins. Robbins had told Sokolow about the dance company and the urgent need to come to Israel and guide its dancers in classic and modern techniques, to prepare them for their tour through Europe and America. In the States Anna Sokolow had become famous for some choreographed pieces she'd composed, the most famous of which was "Rooms". She was a small woman with a fragile appearance that belied her internal fortitude, her powerful, uncompromising personality and her vast artistic knowledge.

During one of our exercises on the floor in a modern dance class, Anna suddenly approached me and pulled my hair to get my body as straight as I could. While pulling my hair she told me to take this profession seriously or trade it for another. No one doubted her seriousness and perfectionism, and very occasionally we managed to get a smile out of her.

Anna Sokolow, Jerome Robbins and Sara Levy-Tanai

Anna Sokolow steadies me in a modern dance class at Inbal

Anna Sokolow at a party with Inbal dancers and parents of dancers

After two years of backbreaking but enjoyable practice under her stern watch, we could feel the difference in the level we'd reached at the end of our work with Anna Sokolow. Each and every dancer's expressive ability had improved drastically, which helped us attain a level of professionalism in the important task Inbal faced with its tour of Europe and America.

Before completing her role at Inbal Anna Sokolow addressed Sara Levy-Tanai and recommended that I continue to give technique classes after she left. It was, without a doubt, an incredible compliment to me. We were all grateful to work with a woman as special and unique as Anna Sokolow.

Inbal members with Anna Sokolow

The Big Tour

It was known that Jerome Robbins had made a recommendation to the American Israeli Cultural Fund and renowned manager **Sol Hurok**, who resided in America, to bring the Inbal dance company in for a six-month tour of the United States, coast-to-coast. We had twelve months to prepare for the trip. The program included "Yemenite Wedding", "The Song of Deborah", "The Queen of Sheba", "Woman of Valor", "Streams in the Desert" and "Shepherd Dances".

The manager Sol Hurok

After a successful three-month tour of Holland, England and Scotland, we boarded the passenger ship SS Amerika at Cove Port in Scotland, and spent a week sailing to New York. The ship was enormous and was considered one of the most luxurious boats in the United States. This fact changed nothing for me as I was bedridden for the entire journey due to seasickness. I was delighted when the ship finally docked at the harbor in New York. I was even happier to feel solid ground beneath my feet. Natural color finally returned to my cheeks.

We arrived at the Fairmont Hotel on W. 58th Street at the center of Manhattan, between Fifth and Sixth Avenue. The hotel was mere minutes away from the Martin Beck Theater where we would perform our shows for three weeks.

On the first day we prepared our first rehearsals on the stage. Those present in the theater included the manager Sol Hurok and the Jewish violinist **Isaac Stern**. At the end of rehearsals Hurok addressed Sara Levy-Tanai and asked her not to use the orchestra accompaniment during the performance and that the dance company members would instead sing along with their dance pieces. This request crashed upon us like thunder on a clear day. After an argument that ended without compromise Hurok threatened to cancel every performance in America and send us back to Israel if we did not do as he demanded. With no alternative, and since it was our first performance, we did as he asked. As someone who had brought the greatest artists from all fields to America, including the best dance companies in the world, Sol Hurok saw Inbal as barely more than a punctuation mark, and he was willing to give us up without a second thought.

Sara Levy with the manager Sol Hurok, listening to Yitzhak Eliezerov playing

At a quarter past seven in the evening the performance began. The early hour was a common practice with every premiere, to allow journalists and art critics to publish their impressions. We eagerly awaited the reviews, and when they came Inbal became an overnight smash hit and global sensation. The critics who had attended the show compared Inbal's artistic style to classic Greece…

The fulsome praise in the press shocked Hurok. It turned out that despite his vast experience in the field of management Hurok had a hard time understanding the audience's taste and demands. He admitted his failure to appreciate Inbal's artistic qualities.

We had achieved incredible success. Jews in the streets of New York recognized us on sight and begged us for tickets to one of their shows, but we couldn't help as every single ticket had been snatched up. I know of one incident with a Jewish family where the mother had gotten a ticket to Inbal in New York, the father saw Inbal in another city and the daughter had to go all the way to Canada for the same.

The success continued throughout the entire tour, which began in the east and continued west, then returned to New York for two more weeks – this time, due to popular demand, at the City Center theater, larger than Martin Beck.

On our way back to Israel the Israeli Ministry of Foreign Affairs asked us to perform a few shows in Scandinavia, Norway, Finland, Sweden and Denmark. The performances, accompanied by famous singer Shoshana Damari, were part of Israel's independence celebrations. Even in Scandinavia Inbal achieved great success.

The tour of Europe, America and Scandinavia lasted nine months. We returned to Israel exhausted but happy. For Sara Levy-Tanai it was a global success. The recognition she received granted her a distinguished position among the most famous choreographers in the world, but it was in no small part due to the members of her dance company that gave her the movement and musical materials which she processed. Later a thick-covered book was published in America that included the top sixteen choreographers who had made their mark on the art of dance. Sara Levy-Tanai was one of them.

Chapter 2

Discovering America

In 1973 far-reaching changes in my life caused my future to take a significant turn. After 19 years of marriage I was forced to separate from my wife and detach myself from my children. I felt I was having difficulties coping with the problems and challenges that accumulated day by day and hour by hour. I felt I was struggling alone and unsuccessfully. I'll admit I didn't have the inner fortitude to withstand all the commitments I'd made. I came to the conclusion that it would be for the best if I left Israel for a while. I believed in the saying "change your place, change your fate", and I had the opportunity to implement that with the Inbal Dance Theater which had been invited to a coast-to-coast tour of the United States. At the time I was a troupe manager in Inbal. During the tour I met and managed contacts with instructors and coordinators in every city in which we performed, and kept the phone numbers as I intended to stay in America at the end of the tour, with the consent of the theater administration.

Before the tour was even finished, I was already receiving invitations to teach dancers on weekends. America welcomed me. My financial situation improved from day to day. The fears that had accompanied me at first vanished, and my self-confidence returned to me. I realized that the idea to temporarily move away from Israel, until the storm passed, was a good decision for me. Financial stability gave me peace of mind, which in turn allowed me to focus on creating without concern. For example, in Israel I had composed dozens of dances in twenty years, whereas in America I composed nearly seventy (!) dances and thirty melodies in fifteen years. A creative person needs mental peace and an encouraging environment, which I didn't have in Israel. My trip to America and my decision to stay and live there granted me a life without worry or restrictions, due to the fact that I could implement anything that came to mind without hesitation and with great satisfaction.

More than once I pondered the life I'd had in Israel, unbearably difficult times where I could not support my family and children. Sometimes I couldn't even bring bread home, even though I played down my problems and shared them with no one, including my family. It never occurred to anyone, even my friends, that talented Moshiko with his unique style might have difficulty supporting his family and children.

Even when I was resolved to leave Israel for a time, to try my luck elsewhere, and word spread among my friends and close relatives, no effort was made to discourage me. Even the Department of Folk Dances with which I'd worked for years, perhaps longer than any other instructor in the country with regards to studios and workshops, took no action in the matter, not even expressing any desire whatsoever. Not that anyone owed it to me, but it was what I secretly wished for.

A Meeting on Gordon Beach

Before leaving for America, in the summer of 1973, I met Gurit Kadman on the beach in Tel-Aviv. Gurit, who lived by Gordon Beach, would exercise and run along the beach, and I would swim out to sea with a group of friends.

When she saw me, Gurit stopped running and began verbally accosting me. She had heard that I was planning to leave Israel and set up shop in America, and said this would damage my Israeli creativity. "The dances you compose will reek of America," she argued. I was silent, how could I know what would really happen in America? Out of respect to Gurit I remained silent. We parted without another word, and Gurit continued her traditional run down the beach.

Workshops in Kfar HaMaccabia

Though I was leaving the country, I kept in constant close contact with Tirtza Hodes. I always kept her informed about my work and experiences in America. Tirtza asked if I might be willing to teach workshops during my visits to Israel which the Department of Folk Dances was arranging at Kfar HaMaccabia. I said yes.

Gurit Kadman had been asked to write up my dance list. When the class was over, she approached me and asked to shake my hand. She said: "Remember our encounter on Gordon Beach, a few days before you left the country? I said some harsh things to you. I want to take back everything I said. Today I've rediscovered you. You've proven that no matter where you live in the world, you'll always remain Moshiko with the same roots we knew in the past. Please forgive me."

I was deeply moved. To hear such warm words from a seventy-five-year-old woman I admired with all my heart was a deeply heartwarming gesture. But that was Gurit's greatness, that she knew how to apologize and that her apologies didn't detract from her personal dignity in the slightest.

After my vacation in Israel I returned to America knowing I had an advocate in Israel in the person of Gurit Kadman. I am blessed to have known her and worked with her.

Is Israeli Creation Possible Outside Israel?

When meeting my fellow professionals in Israel, I explained my side of things regarding leaving the country, and I thank them for their faith in me. One person who "jumped on the bargain" was a senior creator in Israel, who wrote an article for Viltis Magazine which was distributed throughout America, and which contained a harsh attack on Israeli creators living in America, their dances which reeked of the Diaspora, and their entire purpose being profit. This senior also established an organization, supported by the Department of Folk Dances and with the participation of several creators, which chose to boycott any folk dance composed outside the country, especially those composed in America. In an attempt to make this decision a reality gatherings and symposia were held, but in time it became clear that it was "a mountain out of a molehill". The dancing public did not accede to the request of this senior and his associates, with their quixotic tilting at windmills to save the dignity and image of Israeli folk dance. I personally respect each and every one of the members of that group, but utterly reject the idea that they had so much as a leg to stand on, which is why they failed.

Days passed since the senior's article was published in Viltis, and he was invited for a instruction tour in America. The person who arranged these classes was **Yaakov Eden**, an Israeli who had lived in America for quite a few years. Yaakov Eden personally told me how the senior had pushed and pleaded for this American tour.

Yaakov Eden asked the senior to send him a master tape, including the music for the dances he intended to teach in America, in order to print records and sell them at the classes. The recording quality of the music on the master tapes was extremely poor and unprofessional. The dancing public present at the classes, who purchased the record for fifteen dollars, felt cheated. The senior's journey to America ended with a dispute of opinions with Yaakov Eden.

The dancing public in Israel who, at the time, had purchased records from **Moshe Eskayo** and **Shlomo Bachar** and myself, enjoyed the quality and professionalism invested in these recordings at significant financial expense. None of us dared to do in Israel what the senior did to the dancing public in America. If the senior had acted chivalrously and given the dancing public his record at cost, which was at most a dollar per copy, with an apology for its poor quality, this would have been accepted with some esteem. The senior didn't invest so much as a copper penny in the recording, and had not even composed the music himself, nor were the arrangements or production his.

I, on the other hand, sold my records for ten dollars, when my investment for each production came to tens of thousands of dollars! So too were the records of Moshe Eskayo and Shlomo Bachar sold – so who was in fact being indecent and making profit on the backs of the public? The senior's behavior in this case completely contradicted his article in Viltis Magazine. In my opinion, the senior and his associates were wrong in deciding to boycott creators living in America.

Shalom-79 in America

During my stay in America, New York was visited by the dance troupe Shalom-79, managed by **Gavri Levy**. The troupe performed at Radio City, which held about 2,500 seats, but that evening barely 500 people came to the show. It's possible the timing had worked against the troupe – it was some days before Rosh HaShana, when American Jews were busy preparing for the holiday.

The troupe roster included guest artists such as **Arik Lavi**, of blessed memory, and Boaz Sharabi, but the show never "took off" and the disappointed audience began abandoning the theater. I felt horrible. At the end of the show I went backstage to say hello to **Gideon**, an acquaintance from Merchavia Kibbutz, a veteran dancer of the Tzavta Yizrael troupe who had invited me to the show. I told him what had happened in the theater. Gideon passed on my impressions to Gavri Levy, but Gavri did not respond. After the show I returned to my apartment angry, adrenaline coursing through me – this troupe presumed to represent Israel?! I thought to myself disappointedly. I decided to sit down and write to Tirtza Hodes. I told her I was greatly let down by the troupe's performance and awaited her response, but it never came. It then occurred to me that Tirtza herself might have had a part in sending Shalom-79 to America.

Some weeks passed, and a letter arrived from Tirtza. Its content surprised me. Tirtza decided to quote one line from a personal letter I'd sent her, in which I responded to a question she'd asked me about my impression of the new dances recently composed in Israel. My answer to Tirtza's question was: "I believe the creators have reached a dead end, and it would be better for them if they turned to the sources existing in Israel." Tirtza took these words out of context and only used the phrase "the creators have reached a dead end". Moreover, she distributed pamphlets to all creators and instructors, as if to say, "look what Moshiko says about you!" Finally, she asked that responses be sent to the Department of Folk Dances, and it would forward them to me. I was surprised by Tirtza's behavior, finding it difficult to understand how a person could take a letter personally addressed to them and display a line taken from it and distorted in order to embarrass me.

Tirtza hoped that the Department would receive many responses, and indeed they arrived – but only three. The first was from **Giora Kadmon**, of blessed memory, from Merchavia Kibbutz, who wrote thus: "What's this tempest in a teacup? Moshiko has a point, it's just that it's difficult for us to accept criticism from someone who lives outside Israel." The second response came from **Yujo Inbar**, of blessed memory, who wrote: "Moshiko is what we have, and what we live with." There were other lines in that vein, but it certainly wasn't critical towards me. The final response was sharply aggressive and said: "We prefer poor dances composed in Israel than good dances written by an expatriate." It was signed by Jerusalem Studio.

Tirtza was probably comforted by the third response but was certainly disappointed at her companions' disinterest. Most of them preferred to wait until they heard my side of the story.

I came to Israel specially to sort this out. The first thing I did was contact Tirtza and ask to meet her in person. We met at one of the HaPoel Committee buildings and I posed two questions to her: "Where you offended by my letter because of the content pertaining to the Shalom-79 troupe, with which you were connected? Did you intend to present me in a negative light to the dancing and instructor public by presenting my letter to you out of context?" Tirtza's answer to both questions was yes.

Tirtza then admitted that she had made a mistake and apologized to me. Not content with this, she decided to set a meeting at her home with a larger group of friends, to apologize to me in their presence. Unfortunately, only three or four people came to the meeting, myself included, but Tirtza's apology and her asking me for forgiveness was respectable.

The Double Album

I flew to America with four masters in my suitcase containing the music which accompanied my dances, hoping I could make a single-cover double album out of them.

With the conclusion of Inbal's tour in America, I began the work of producing the double album. The man who assisted me in producing the album was **Fred Berk**, who lived in America and was considered a dominant force in the field of Israeli folk dancing.

Within a month the double album was published and gained unusual success due to its musical quality. The request for the album exceeded expectation. I had invested a considerable amount of money from my perspective – fifteen thousand dollars, but the investment proved worthwhile. Within a year I'd made it all back. This reminds me of a story that took place earlier, while I was still in Israel.

A few years before leaving the country, I approached the Department of Folk Dances with an offer to produce an album with the melodies which accompanied my dances. Since they had a distinct Eastern character, I asked to head up the project, as this would allow me to choose the proper arranger and musicians who could be trusted with the special traits and styles of the melodies. I notified them in advance that I sought no compensation for my work, I simply wanted the dancing public to be accompanied by music performed on instruments that could express the style and character of the dance. My proposal was rejected due to a lack of funding. What's interesting is that some time before my request was made, the Department of Folk Dances had produced an album for Rivka Sturman. Anyone would have felt slighted by this.

In 1975, after two years in America, I came back to Israel with two more records under my belt, a third and fourth that I had recorded after my double album. Each contained twelve new compositions for new dances.

Instructing and Composing

The classes I gave across America multiplied. Weekends were packed with multiple requests, so that even in the middle of the week I was teaching almost every day. Despite the massive pressure, I felt significant material satisfaction.

Over time I decided to stick with weekend instruction only, to use weekdays for matters pertaining to dance, composition and other hobbies, like painting, which gave me excitement and pleasure.

For fifteen years I "worked" America's length and breadth, reaching most dancing groups, including groups that mainly performed international folk dances. Personally, I enjoyed teaching those groups, with their dancers' vast experience in different styles of dance which allowed them to execute my own dances with great precision and enjoyment.

Their opinions of Israeli folk dances thus far had not been particularly positive. They claimed most Israeli dances were superficial and lacked a sense of roots. But when they were exposed to my dances they felt, in their own words, that my dances were based on ethnic elements drawn from the rich cultural and ethnic elements in Israel.

Globe-Spanning Connections

In my journey around the world I've represented Israel, and the impression I left opened up a system of connections and invitations for future visits. For example, in London I spent twenty-six consecutive years as an instructor at Machol Europa, the largest of all dance camps in Europe. In fact, I was among those who came up with the idea of establishing the camp along with **Maurice and Suzie Stone**; in Belgium I participated in Machol Aviv and Machol Choref for twenty-five consecutive years; three years at Hora New York; six years at Hora Shalom in New York; eight years at Hora Keff in New York; I visited Japan twelve times in twenty years; it would be enough for me to name America, Europe, Australia and New Zealand, Japan, Taiwan, Russia, Ukraine and the Czech Republic. I suppose that had it not been for the unique style that characterized my dances I would not have earned the respect and esteem that the dancing public in Israel and worldwide granted me, and continues to grant to this day.

Fred Berk – My Man in America

I first met Fred Berk, among the leaders of Israeli folk dancing in America, in the summer of 1971 while he was staying in Israel with a group of young Americans who had come to visit the country and learn its dances. The group was staying at Kfar HaMaccabia, where Israeli folk dance creators were invited. Fred came to visit the Inbal studio to meet Sarah Levy-Tanai, as well as to speak with me about the possibility of coming to instruct his group. In the same conversation he said that he had tried to contact me before, but I'd been staying abroad at the time.

I was impressed by Fred's personality. Even after teaching his group we continued meeting and talking every now and then. I felt he had taken a special interest in my dances and appreciated my approach and perception with regards to Israeli folk dances. I drew encouragement from his words and from the fact that a man in his position respected my work, learned my dances and even taught and spread them across the United States.

In 1972 and 1973, I was again invited to teach when he arrived in Israel with different groups. The relationship between us grew stronger and I felt I could trust him when our conversations turned to more general matters.

In 1973, the night Inbal departed for its tour of the United States, I told Fred about my preparations for the trip and revealed him that at the end of the tour I planned to stay in America. I wanted to know what he thought of this, and to what extent he might be willing to help me find my place there. Fred said he would do his best to help me with instructing across the nation, after my relationship with Inbal came to its end. He even gave me his address and phone number, while I still had no permanent apartment, but in return he asked me to be a guest instructor at Blue Star Dance Camp which he organized every June. Of course I was happy to accept. It was a great honor to be invited to work with Fred Berk at one of the most famous dance camps in America. I eagerly awaited the day.

Inbal's tour began on October 7 1973 on the West Coast, and gradually moved east. In most of the states we performed, I met dance instructors who dealt with Israeli folklore and was invited to teach my dances. I was surprised by the desire of teachers and dancers to meet me and study my dances, which had been composed in Israel and had become so popular in America. Two months later, on the 8th of December, my contract with Inbal was at its end. The very next day I began moving across the continent, according to invitations I'd received – some of which had been mediated by Fred Berk.

In the meanwhile, I rented an apartment with a phone, so that we were in almost-daily contact. Fred accompanied me to various offices regarding the production of my double album.

Prior to that, in Israel, Fred had explained to me that success in the United States depended on me bringing professionally recorded music with me. I did as he said. I pulled together the necessary funds and approached **Albert Piamente**, known musician and arranger, to complete the task. These recordings, the fulfillment of a years-long dream, ended with me possessing a master tape of the first twenty dances I'd composed in fourteen years – from 1959 to 1973.

Fred Berk behind, myself on his right side, with two students who'd invited us to teach on a weekend in Philadelphia

We brought the master tapes to the offices of **Gary Harris**, Fred Berk's friend and assistant, who was also in the business of producing albums. By the end of the meeting I felt my plans coming together, so unlike the difficulty I'd encountered in Israel.

Things progressed at a dizzyingly fast pace. 1974 was overflowing with activity to the point that I couldn't withstand the number of requests made to me. It was an important recovery in my life, and well-rewarding.

The Dance Festival at Madison Square Garden

In February 1974 the Israeli Folk Dance Festival was held at Madison Square Garden. Fred Berk invited me to instruct the Yehuda HaTza'ir movement's dance group, which consisted of young dancers who lacked experience in the field of dance but had a strong will to face the challenge head-on. The work included stage choreography named Ki Hivshiloo Eshkolot. Mere days before the Festival, Fred invited all the participating bands to the Y (the Jewish Community Center on 92nd Street in Manhattan), to review them and provide feedback. When he saw my choreography with the Yehuda HaTza'ir dancers, there was an expression of enjoyment and satisfaction on his face, and at the end of rehearsals he complimented me on my work.

The festival was a smashing success. I felt that, like many others, I too had contributed to that success. A few days later Fred and I traveled to Philadelphia for a weekend to teach Israeli folk dances at the University of Pennsylvania. Most of the work was based on me. Fred only provided a lecture and showed a film on the Dalia Festival in Israel. I wasn't bothered by this; I didn't even know the amount I'd receive for this work. As we were returning to New York by train, Fred gave me my paycheck. Only later did I learn from the organizers that the sum I was meant to receive was considerably higher than what Fred had given me.

During the train ride I felt that Fred was acting different. I tried to get him talking to find out what had happened, and then he told me he thought he would stop teaching. I felt that perhaps I was the reason for his decision, because who could teach Moshiko dances besides Moshiko himself? I asked him not to consider it and said I was willing to work with him at every opportunity. I even considered presenting this to the organizers as a precondition, but Fred didn't respond. We reached New York and promised to stay in contact via phone before going our separate ways.

Despite my considerable workload, I found opportunities to visit the Y on Wednesdays, to see Fred and admire his ability to "conduct" the dances, despite one of his legs being impaired. The atmosphere was full of youthful glee. The dancers adored Fred. At the end of his workday we would sit in the small room next to the dance hall that also served as his office and discuss all sorts of issues pertaining to our common profession. Fred had already announced that I would be participating in Blue Star, but he hadn't let me know and the matter was a complete mystery to me. My interest was huge and full of curiosity, I wanted to know how matters were going at the camp and what the work plan was. Fred explained to me that when a guest instructor was present, he would teach in a different hall and the dancing public would choose who to dance with. It seemed a bit odd to me, as this would create competition between the instructors. I was worried about getting caught up in a situation where since Fred was so well-known for so many years, and I was a relative newcomer, the dancers might be more curious about my classes. When I explained this to Fred his answer was that if my theory proved true he would go to sleep. Only later, after we parted ways, did I reconsider the whole matter and conclude that it had been a mistake to bring it up, that I should let time run its course. I hoped time would scatter the fog between us.

Misunderstanding and Crisis

Two weeks had passed and I again dropped by for a visit at the Y. I was upbeat and eagerly awaited the end of the dance. I wanted to share my experiences over the past two weeks with Fred, but even before the evening was over Fred asked one of the dancers to replace him and asked me to accompany him. We went to his office.

As soon as I walked in, Fred began speaking very harshly towards me, accusing me of speaking poorly of him. I needed a few minutes to understand what he was even talking about, and what he was trying to say. I sat there stunned, unable to process what was happening. I didn't understand why Fred was speaking to me so harshly and insultingly. Tears welled up in my eyes and I asked Fred to at least tell me who was making up stories about me. Fred Berk evaded the question.

It was a difficult pill to swallow. I couldn't believe the man I so admired and respected was treating me this way. When he sensed how deeply I was offended Fred asked me to forget the whole thing and that we start over. He asked me to walk him to his apartment nearby, and then apologized again. I went back to my room and couldn't sleep, my eyes refused to close. I saw dawn breaking past the curtain of my window and only then, at sunrise, did I fall asleep.

A week later I found a letter waiting for me in my mailbox. It was from Fred Berk, who was vacationing in California. I opened the letter, which said something to the extent of:

> *To Moshiko,*
>
> *I've reconsidered the incident between us and I don't think I can continue collaborating with you. I am therefore revoking your participation at Camp Blue Star.*
>
> *I appreciate your work and to me you are the premier creator of Israeli folk dances. I hope we can stay in touch despite no longer working together. I'll call you when I return to New York.*
>
> *Fred Berk*

I had decided to give Fred another chance after the first unjustified "backstab", and not jump to conclusions, but this time, especially after Fred had apologized and asked to start over, I was unwilling to compromise. I decided to cut off all contact with him.

When he returned from California, he tried to call me, and left messages asking me to get back to him, but I ignored them. Fred sent me two letters to which I also did not respond, letting him understand that a reasonable person does not leave his back open to a third knife. Fred tried again and again to renew contact but in vain, until he got the message and stopped trying.

When he returned to New York from a work tour in California, I traveled there for a period of three months, teaching on the West Coast of the United States. It was clear to me that during his stay in California Fred had met with **Israel Yakovee**, who was just starting out as a dance instructor, and decided to incorporate him into Camp Blue Star instead of me. Though he had at least two months at his disposal, Fred didn't change the content of the Blue Star advertisements and preferred to just declare the facts in the field.

I was surprised by his decision; as someone who knew him well I knew how much he insisted on perfection and quality above all else, and here he had ignored these two values that were so important to him.

When I met Israel Yakovee, I asked whether he intended to teach my dances at Blue Star. He said yes, and I made it clear that I did not approve and I might not allow him to participate in my classes. Israel recanted and promised he wouldn't teach my dances, unless it was at the general dances in the evenings, and in accordance with the dancers' wishes. He promised to base his classes on the dances of Shlomo Bachar, in coordination with Fred Berk. Here again, I couldn't understand the contradiction in Fred's behavior. I was quite familiar with his negative opinion about Israeli creators living in America and creating Israeli folk dances. Fred never hesitated to use any means to make those Israelis' lives difficult and hobble their steps. As evidence, I never heard a single Israeli who dealt with Israeli folk dancing say a good word about Fred Berk. He wanted exclusive control of the field of Israeli dances. I don't question his contribution – he did much to glorify Israel's reputation in America in the field of folk dancing, but at the same time he acted arbitrarily and aggressively with people who were no less sensitive than him, as though Israeli folkdancing were his private property.

Blue Star Without Me

I acknowledged and cherished Fred's contribution to Israeli folk dancing, but I couldn't avoid noticing his behavior. Over time I came to understand I wasn't his only victim, others had been hurt by him to the depths of their souls. I never took an interest, never asked or investigated, it didn't matter to me, but those people I would accidentally run into would unload their hearts' burdens onto me. I learned that Fred had hurt a great many people, even those who adored him and dedicated so much of their time to his needs.

With the deterioration of our friendship I decided not to visit the Y any more – the wound hadn't yet healed and it followed me everywhere. Friends who tried to get me to talk about it and present my case returned empty-handed. "Ask Fred," I'd say. "Maybe he'll give you an answer that'll put you at ease."

The day the Blue Star camp opened I was inundated with phone calls. When the participants found out I wouldn't be involved with the camp they turned to Fred, but his answers were unsatisfying. They hoped to hear from me. I'll never forget their sob-choked voices when they realized I wouldn't be coming to the camp. They felt cheated as no one had bothered to inform them in advance. Rumors had spread among all the dancers, many wanted explanations, but Fred got tangled up in his replies – he told some I was sick and therefore unable to participate; he told others I hadn't come due to a disagreement; and others still were told it was a personal matter between us and he couldn't comment.

Ultimately the camp was a success, mostly because of the evening dances, and due to the great demand to perform my dances, so I was told by Israel Yakovee. Some even agreed to stay long after the dance to learn more from Israel, particularly my new dances. Though Fred was not on site he knew what was happening in that dance hall. I think if he could have prevented the public from dancing my dances he would have done so without hesitation, but he knew such a decision would be a grave mistake.

Five Years Later

As the years passed Fred's health deteriorated, and his activity was limited. He gave up the Wednesday dances at the Y among various other activities. **Ruth Goodman**, one of his students, and **Danny Uziel** took his place. Fred decided to dedicate his time to research and writing about Israeli dance. He wanted to do as much as possible, time had become a vital commodity for him.

Despite the disconnect between us I was sorry to hear of Fred's medical condition, but in light of the difficult incident we'd experienced there was nothing I could do about it. Fred and I remained out of contact for five years.

One Wednesday I felt like stopping by the Y. When I got there, after so long a period where I hadn't visited, I was surprised to see Fred Berk sitting by the stage. I imagine he was just as surprised to see me. I deliberated whether to stay or go, but decided to stay and face the problem. After all – it had been five years since the incident. I was greeted at the Y warmly, feeling loved and wanted, and I tried to ignore Fred's presence.

I walked into the hall and had just gotten comfortable when Danny Uziel walked up to me and said: "Since Fred's already here, why don't you talk to him, Moshiko? Shake hands and make up." I told Danny I was the injured party, and politely refused his suggestion. Suddenly Fred stood up, walked over to me and held out his hand. I did the same, and we shook hands. Fred invited me to his home.

On the day of the visit I was quite emotional, unclear on how we could close a five-year-gap and act as though nothing had happened.

Fred greeted me warmly. We sat across from each other and he asked not to speak of the past. "We've already wasted five years," he noted. He said he was sorry for our long alienation and said how much he respected me and considered me a premier creator. He told me that he had followed my work over the past five years, and was impressed with my new dances. Finally he admitted that his fear that America would interfere with the originality of my work proved to be complete fiction.

I told Fred I was gathering material for a book on my experience in the field of dance and my integration into the Israeli folkdance enterprise, my work with minority troupes and more. Fred was greatly interested and wanted us to discuss it further. I asked if he would be willing to write the introduction to my book, he was deeply moved and said it was a great compliment to him and he would gladly do so.

I let out a relieved breath, noticing that Fred's health had improved after his chemotherapy, and his illness seemed to be in remission. I felt happiness beaming from Fred's face and that he was getting ready to come back to his favorite activity with gusto. He had to fly to Florida for recuperation, but when he came back, so he said, he would be happy for us to meet.

We parted warmly, hoping to see each other as soon as he got back from Florida. I could never have imagined that would be our last meeting. In his will Fred asked to be cremated, which prevented his friends from escorting him on his last journey.

Some months before Fred's death, he felt his end approaching. He asked to meet the Israeli dance instructors working in America, to ask their forgiveness. He wanted to die with a clean conscience, but it was such a shame, all those wasted years where so much suffering and stinging pain could have been prevented.

May his memory be a blessing!

Blue Star Camp teaching staff

Chapter 3

On Choreographers of Israeli Folk Dances in America

More than sixty years ago, young Israelis started making their way to the United States of America with the goal of improving their quality of life. Among them were a handful of Physical Education teachers, while others had a background and experience in folk dancing, and some came with artistic experience. Given a lack of opportunities for income, these young people decided to focus on Israeli folk dances.

By then the State of Israel had already gained its independence, and the American public's attitude towards it and its people was warm and sympathetic. This attitude stood out from the Jews' point of view. Every Israeli arriving in the States was greeted with open arms. The Jewish youth at cultural centers like the JCC found in Israeli folk dancing a means to identify with the struggles of Israel and the people residing there.

This sympathy was a good reason for those youths to decide they were worthy of representing and spreading Israeli folk dancing across America, and the American people never challenged or questioned their capabilities.

Only the aforementioned Fred Berk, an authority on Israeli folk dances, refused to accept this fact (as the Israelis themselves later revealed). Fred did everything in his power to prevent those Israeli youths from receiving aid that would allow them to work in the field of Israeli folk dances, which was under his control and influence in America. The Israelis, for their part, stubbornly refused to give in, on the contrary, they enriched themselves by studying a large number of folk dances, and each established a place where they could work: Dani Dassa and Shlomo Bachar, in Los Angeles in California, were later joined by Israel Yakovee. Moshe Eskayo worked in New York and was joined by Danny Uziel. At the end of 1973 I joined the New York area. We all taught folk dancing, to the benefit of the dancing public, and we all earned our income respectably.

Over time the instructors began composing their own original folk dances, but these were attached to existing melodies that accompanied dances composed in Israel. The phenomenon created duplicates that only embarrassed the dancing public. The American dancers who came to Israel and joined the circle discovered that in Israel there was a version that was different than the one they'd learned, and vice versa, Israelis arriving in America learned there was an American version of that same familiar tune. I felt uncomfortable due to the dancers' embarrassment.

When I established myself in the States, I noticed this phenomenon, alerted others to it and expressed my dissatisfaction. I also felt an injustice was being done to Israeli folk dances by these choreographers living in America who were ignoring everything happening in Israel. As a result, they were not acknowledged by the Division of Folk Dances in Israel and to some extent they were even boycotted. Sadly, this negative habit continued indifferently. However, and I say this with great sadness, there were also choreographers in Israel who used melodies composed specifically for dances composed in America, and I see them as equally guilty of being unfair towards their fellow professionals as well as the dancing public and the image of Israeli folk dancing. This behavior from my fellow professionals contributed nothing before and was equally unhelpful now. Everyone was entitled to compose Israeli folk dances so long as it was constructive and not destructive, especially if they had the talent, the skill and the internal urge to compose.

Over the years largely negative competitions were held among Israeli choreographers and instructors living in America. Each wanted to succeed, even at the expense of another. The dancing public felt this negative atmosphere and it was a subject of daily conversation at every meeting.

After some years in America and touring the country I discovered some of the new dances that had been attached to new melodies, the quality of which were better than some dances composed in Israel. The American dancing public, and later the Israeli dancing public, received them warmly. My impression was that Israeli criticism of Israeli dance choreographers operating in America derived primarily from jealousy, because the Torah had not come from Zion after all. It would have been better if the Israeli choreographers had taken on the collective responsibility and the acceptable demands, within the framework of Israel's Division of Folk Dances, to remain in constant contact with the Division and provide information on any new dances and music composed in America. I personally did so during all my years there, in order to prevent duplicates. I also maintained my connection with the dancing and instructing public with my every visit to Israel, when I would be asked to teach my new dances which earned me significant recognition from all parties.

But this reflects the zeitgeist of the seventies and eighties, when the Division of Folk Dances still operated. Unfortunately, the Division is now defunct and in fact there is no official body to collaborate with at all. Still, looking back, we can acknowledge that the Israeli choreographers who lived and are still living in America contributed and enriched the repertoire of Israeli folk dances which became an "inalienable asset" to Israel and worldwide, and I'm proud to note their names here:

Dani Dassa and his dances: Joshua, Rachel, Shedemati, and Ashrei HaIsh

Moshe Eskayo and his dances: Ramot, Debka Allon, Debka Keff, Dagidi, HaShir Sheli, Livavteenee, Shir HaChatuna, Liya, and Debka Li'el

Danny Uziel and his dances: At V'Ani and HaNokdim (composed in Israel)

Shlomo Bachar and his dances: Eretz Eretz, Tfila, and Shir HaShirim

Israel Yakovee and his dances: Shoofni, Abba Shimon, Achot Lanu Ktana, Shavnu, Yemenite Rap, and Agadelcha

Benny Levy and his dances: Tzel Etz Tamar and Debka Benyamin

Naftali Kadosh and his dances: Nishar Itach, Zara, Mischak HaDma'ot, Debka Nufar, Debka Etti, Debka Dikla, Le'ehov Im Efshar, and Ahava Yam Tichonit

This is just a small selection from a large and rich repertoire, and it would be an injustice to claim it reeks of Diaspora. You can feel the unique Israeli-Tsabar roots in each of these dances.

Yes to Creators – No to the Impulse

The eighties were a low point in a way. The choreographers in Israel were complacent in the field of creation and the dancing public was thirsty for new material, new dances, and thus an opportunity appeared to fill the void.

The Israeli choreographers living in America would visit Israel and were invited to teach their dances in workshops or dance nights across the country, reaping great success. All the dances composed in America are still performed to this day, and doubtless will continue to be danced for many years to come. It was clear that their connection to Israel had never stopped for a moment, and with their departure from the country they had taken their roots with them, as was evident from the dances they composed.

There is no Israeli critique of choreographers living in America anymore, it has become a fact of life. It took time to understand that this criticism had no receptive audience and was nothing more than a futile falsehood.

Israeli culture does not exclusively feed off artists who live in Israel, but also off Jewish and non-Jewish artists living outside the country, including Israeli artists living abroad. All these contribute with love and continue to do so for Israeli culture. I hope the day will come when we know to honor and appreciate each other out of mutual respect. Let's encourage our own inner creative spirits and not let the negative impulse overtake us.

Part C
Thoughts and Opinions

a. Sources of and Influences on Israeli Folk Dance

From the very beginning choreographers of Israeli folk dances drew inspiration both from their origins – the Hassidic and Yemenite dance – and the pioneering spirit of the working settlements – the Israeli dance. Another influence that had significant effect on the style of Israeli folkdances is the Arab "Debka".

The aforementioned four ethnic groups – Hassidic, Yemenite, Israeli and Arab – had tremendous impact on the character of Israeli folk dances. Each group has its own style and distinct impetus for being created.

In **Hassidic dance** the mystical sensation pent up within the body is especially evident. The dancer draws energy from the periphery into their body. Through dance, the dancer's soul ascends to connect with the divine spirit.

The Hassidic dance consists of four phases:

1. Prelude – playing the clarinet with no rhythm (confession)

2. The dance – beginning the rhythm

3. The ecstasy – increasing the rhythm to its climax

4. The conclusion

The Hassidic dance is in fact a ritual – a prayer to God through movement. However, unlike the ritual dances of other ethnic groups (African, for example), this ritual dance does not rob the dancer of consciousness.

The **Yemenite dance** and the Hassidic dance have common ground pertaining to the structure and development of the dance. The Yemenite dancer executes light movements and hovers above the ground. They do not place their full weight on the ground, as the ground of Yemen is temporary, not sanctified like the land of Israel. Throughout all the years of exile the Yemenite community believed life in Yemen was temporary, and in their prayers they hoped redemption would come soon. Indeed, the prophecy came true, as it was written: "And He will gather the dispersed of Judah from the four corners of the earth on the wings of eagles." There is no question that culturally, artistically, kinesthetically and musically, the Yemenite ethnic group contributed not only to folk dancing, but to all of Israeli culture, immeasurably more so than any other ethnic group in the country.

The **Israeli dance** presents a Tzabar style with an open and confident chest, shoulders straight and head held high and proud. This is a new generation that did not know, or want to know, what exile was. In terms of choreographic structure, the Israeli dance takes up more space, and unlike the Hassidic and Yemenite dances its movements are larger and broader. The Israeli dance uses internal energy and explodes outward with it, to the periphery, while in Hassidic and Yemenite dance the energy is drawn from the periphery inward, towards the body. The Israeli folk dance today has achieved global success.

Debka ("Dabke") means "stamping" in Arabic. The **Arab Debka** contributed significantly to our line dances and influenced them. In the debka dance we experience the connection between a farmer and his land. The dance is based on stamping one's feet in a variety of paces and emphases. Usually only men dance the debka, and every group has a leader who stands at the head and leads it. The group executes its movements based on the **leader**'s instructions, in unison, as one, with the outstanding characteristic being the internal discipline of each participant.

Every leader has the privilege of leaving the line and improvising as they see fit, while the group continues to carry out the movements as instructed. The debka expresses a rustic lifestyle. Every village has a leader and the village residents are in fact one large family consisting of fathers, mothers, brothers and sisters, uncles and aunts, and relatives of various degrees. Each such village chooses a leader according to whom all things are arranged. The leader is involved in all aspects of the village's daily life – the legislator and sole arbiter in crucial decisions relating to the village residents. We see this in the debka as well, a consolidated and disciplined group for the leader – something that characterizes daily life in the village.

6. Origins of Yemenite Dance and its Influence on Israeli Culture

As far back as the days of the First Temple, as the prophet Zachariah foretold of the coming ruin and the great invasion of Israel, the tribes of Judah and Levy were the only ones that accepted the prophet's warning and went into exile before the land was destroyed. During their departure, they took with them everything they could carry, and turned their eyes to what lay beyond the Jordan river. While crossing the river they continued along nearly the same route Moses had followed to bring the people of Israeli to the Promised Land after their exodus from Egypt.

The journey took several years, at the end of which they arrived at the place currently known as Yemen – one of the most ancient states in the world. Yemen has many names: Maayan, Sheba, taken from the marvelous story of the Queen of Sheba who tried to entrap King Solomon with riddles but could not resist him; Kotban and Himiar – all these until the rise of the warlord **Ali**, a relative of the prophet Mohammed who defeated the Turks and conquered the entire area. There is a plausible theory that Ali was the one who named the country **Yemen**.

The Jews who built their homes in this area were called Yemenites, but they never forgot their Jewish roots for a moment. In their eyes, Yemen was a transitory place, with their eyes always turned to the land of their forefathers. Thus, they made sure to carefully maintain the Jewish religious life and traditions, study the Torah and keep its mitzvoth, and keep the family pure by not assimilating into the foreign nation.

This zealous protection of religion was a fearsome defense against any negative influence on the lives of Jews in Yemen. To our joy, the Jews of Yemen managed to preserve their rich and unique folklore, including songs in Hebrew that apparently were sung during exile, in the age of the First Temple; prayers and chants; and a rich cache of movements expressing longing for the land of their forefathers – Israel itself. The harsh restrictions placed upon them for centuries were expressed in the small dance movements, being focused and carried out almost in place, with the emphasis on the motion of the hands and body. In contrast, Jews living outside the capital, in less populated areas including the mountains, moved freely and expressively.

For many years the Jews of Yemen dreamed of returning to Israel, and the holy city of Jerusalem, according to the words of the prophet, "on eagle's wings". In their rich imagination they longed for that awaited day when they could return to the rock from which they had been hewn. And indeed, their dream and the prophet's vision materialized fully in 1949-1950. Their ears could not believe the words of the Imam, the king of Yemen, who gave the Jews permission to leave his country. It was doubly joyous for Israel, as on the one hand – Israel had triumphed in the War of Independence and defeated the Arab nations who had taken part in their war against Israel, and on the other hand – it was the consummation of an ancient dream after two thousand years of exile in the Diaspora. Upon leaving Yemen the Jews left all their property behind so as not to be burdened and thus delay their return to Israel. Some of their glorious assets, the richest in the culture, which included among other things ancient Torah books, were lost, as were the money and gold which were buried in secret places and left behind. Boarding the giant planes, which seemed to them like eagles, the Jews of Yemen took with them only meager bundles, and when they arrived in Israel, they lay flat upon the holy ground and kissed it.

Upon their arrival they scattered throughout the country, establishing new settlements largely based on working the land and raising chickens and livestock. Due to the enclosed lifestyle they had known, they faced many difficulties in adjusting, but slowly began integrating themselves into life in Israel. The hesitation and anxiety vanished, and the young generation began to involve themselves in local life. Their rich culture, expressed in gold and silver artistry, found a tremendous audience and many admirers. Their dances and songs served as inspiration for a comprehensive research on this interesting and unique community, with a charm that drew every eye to it. Their traditions, customs and vibrant dance movements found their way into the world of Israeli folk dancing, which was just starting to coalesce. Folk dancing, until that time, was a collection of borrowed movements from other countries and peoples which the first pilgrims had brought with them upon their arrival in Israel. These movements were decorated with Israeli melodies and little originality, but with significant vision, the joy of life and love of the homeland.

The various ceremonies, celebrations and festivals were central events and a golden opportunity for the entire dancing public to enjoy the experience of dancing together. With every year that passed the number of dancers grew, and with it the hunger for something more original in Israeli dance increased.

c. The Contribution of Yemenite Steps to Israeli Dance

The Yemenite Step is just one drop of water in the oceanic contribution the Yemenite ethnic group bestowed upon Israeli culture since coming to Israel during the "Magic Carpet" operation in 1949-1950. Their customs, traditions, and especially their vibrant dance moves found their way to the world of Israeli folk dance, which at the time was in its infancy, with a narrow collection of steps borrowed from all sorts of cultures that had come to us from Russia, Eastern Europe, Germany and more. What was so special about Yemenite steps that so charmed and fascinated those that dealt with folk dance? Few suspected that beyond the formal and technical structure of Yemenite movements lay mystery, subtlety, lightness, and beauty, which created a special style of dance.

If I'm not mistaken, the first to take an interest and find use for Yemenite steps was the dancer and choreographer Yardena Cohen, z"l, one of the pioneers of dance; after her came Sarah Levy-Tanai, z"l, founder of the Inbal dance theater, who used her artistic talents to turn the Yemenite dance steps into a global phenomenon; after them came Rivka Sturman, z"l, among the pioneering creators of folk dances, and Gurit Kadman, z"l, a creator who was among the founders of the folk dance movement in Israel.

The Yemenite step was a central ingredient in almost every Israeli folk dance and gave our folk dances the Israeli identity in the world. The rich Yemenite step enriched our local dance language, captured the gaze of any who saw it, and challenged every dancer.

A Challenge for Every Dancer – Why?

The rhythm of the Yemenite step is based on 4/4, but it is executed in three steps while shifting the body's weight from one side to the other, followed by a pause. Some might think the step is simple in structure and form, but I have an anecdote about this.

One day, back when I was one of Inbal's dancers, we invited one of the most famous ballet troupes in the world to our studio, the London Festival Ballet from England, which had come to perform a series of shows in Israel with world-renowned soloists. After presenting several pieces to them, we invited them to a dance circle at a Yemenite rhythm. All they had to do was – a Yemenite step. It was funny to see English dancers struggle to cope with the Yemenite step and shifting their body from side to side, including the head dancer **John Gilpin** who was very embarrassed. That same famous dancer – who could execute two spins in the air and softly land on his knee or do three spins on one leg – couldn't carry out the supposedly simple, humble and introverted Yemenite step. Over time, in light of the success of the Yemenite step and its integration into folk dance, many stories have been woven around it to strengthen it, such as the notion that the lightness of motion and contact with the soles of the feet were meant to stay airborne as long as possible, so as not to touch foreign soil…

From the very beginnings of our folk dance to this very day, young and talented choreographers belonging to that ethnic group have added many Yemenite movement-related elements, in different variations, which have enriched the language of our dance with beauty and quality.

Today, with Israeli folk dances performed around the world and wildly successfully, there are barely any Israeli folk dances that don't have the Yemenite step. The Yemenite step is a vital foundational component in the existing cache of movements, and it enriches our folk dances with its unique visual beauty.

d. Am I a Creator or a Choreographer?

Despite being counted among creators in the field of folk dancing, I have absolute reservations regarding the title **creator**. To me the word connects with God, the Creator and Maker, and who are we to compare ourselves to Him?

The Committee on behalf of the Division of Folk Dances erred during discussions on the definition of dance choreographers by deciding to call them **creators**, without establishing criteria as to who deserved such a title. The Committee similarly erred in not organizing a schedule by which each candidate would be tested, a least for a certain period, in order to prove that their talents were indeed based on personal accomplishments which justified the bestowing of such a title, or that said talent was nothing more than a passing phenomenon. The title of creator is a binding obligation, setting a high standard that none of us have yet to reach in the field of folk dances. Thus, it is proper and worthy that we cease thinking of folk dances as "creations" or artistic masterpieces. Our folk dances must be of the folk, foundational, ethnic, with some message, so that the dancing public can identify with it.

No **choreographer** can elevate their dance to the level of a creation, with structured comprising two parts or two parts and a chorus, when the dance is a minute or a minute and a half long. Of course, this does not apply when the creation is meant for the stage and its content is artistic rather than for the folk.

The creator creates ex nihilo, while we feed off what exists. To this day none of us have invented or created some movement that has never been used before. We all benefit from existing materials. There is no better testament to this than observing our dances. Most resemble each other because they are based on the same elements, organized differently. Where is the creation here?

I am aware of the fact that some of our dances are "indispensable assets", and we enjoy dancing them for their dance structure and the interesting combination of movement and music. And yet this is neither a creation nor a masterpiece, but merely a correct coincidence. At the same time, a choreographer cannot foresee success or failure for the dance that has been composed, and most of us have experimented with dances that saw the light of day and died within days or weeks.

With all our goodwill, all we're trying to do is compose dances in a variety of levels and qualities – some turn out well while others don't. It all depends on the personality, the artistic cultural baggage and our – choreographers' – sense of self-criticism. Dances that disappear only prove they were not made of the stuff rooted in the traditions, origins and values that grant a dance immortality.

And so, as a gesture of respect for the title **creator**, let us humbly settle for the term choreographers, and not see the definition of **choreographer** as inferior, flawed or a disadvantage. This title respects those who hold it and still demands responsibility and commitment.

If we do our work loyally, we will earn the sympathy, praise, respect and esteem that everyone wishes for.

e. Quantity versus Quality

The folk dancing public in Israel has grown on a daily basis. Classes are bursting with dancers, the instructors are enjoying their work and we are all satisfied – after all, these were our dreams and our hearts' desires all these years. The dancers form a large movement that has taken a place of honor in Israeli culture, and its influence is significant abroad as well.

While it's true that this reality gives us much satisfaction and encourages us to continue along this path, it also raises an important problem we haven't responded to, especially in the last fifteen years: the **quality** of the material.

Unfortunately, if we've succeeded in our first task we've certainly failed in our second. As the years pass the gap between **quantity** and **quality** grows, even though the subject has been discussed extensively in meetings and symposia. Practically speaking, nothing has been done to balance the situation and we stand helpless and unable to deal with the problem.

Moreover, to my great regret, I fear we have "missed the boat". I don't want to sound pessimistic, but in light of the current reality I don't see any solution in the future that would assuage concerns, and why?

a. The problematic quality of the material does not stem from an individual but is shared by all those who work in this field, with no exceptions.

b. The lack of consensus among all those currently active in the field is the main reason no solution has been found for the problem.

c. Another reason that prevents us from implementing specific qualities in our work is the fact that our folk dancing movement is run like an industrial cartel, overseen by entrepreneurs who are chiefly concerned with their personal interests and profit. May my friends and associates forgive me if my words are too harsh, I don't mean to offend anyone, but I must note the fact that nobody connected to the folk dancing movement in Israel is doing so for ideological-Zionist reasons. However, I can certainly understand that there's nothing wrong with making a living off this profession.

d. There is another factor, to my understanding, that prevents us from reaching that level of necessary quality, which is the sheer quantitative mass of the dancing public, and a certain measure of consent on the part of instructors who do not see the quality of the material as an important precondition to dealing with folk dances.

For the first few years of folk-dance activity in Israel, everything operated on a small scale. The dances and workshops took place in small groups with a limited number of participants. In these circumstances supervision and control was possible. Over time, as the dancing movement in Israel grew, we lost control, and in the absence of a leader with any influence – we lost our restraint.

The first generation, on whose laps we were educated, was gone without leaving heirs to lead with the same wisdom and insight they had had. The second generation managed to make it through the melting pot and was very influenced by the first generation. Its qualitative contribution was immeasurable, but this generation is also thinning out and leaving us.

The current generation has disavowed the era of the pioneers. To them, Zionism belongs to the history books, and they have no interest in the deeper meaning of roots and origins. This generation is more independent, more interested in "here and now" than "yesterday". Its productions are influenced by what's happening in their immediate surroundings, through unlimited use of elements of modern movement combined with classical techniques to improve operational abilities.

The source of this influence stems from the professional stage, from professional dance troupes, whether local or international, as well as from different styles with no restrictions, limits or distinction. The roots of ethnic folklore are not a source of inspiration for this generation to utilize, and that's a pity. It must be noted that a small portion of contemporary choreographed works that service our folklore characterize a new way and approach that expresses itself on stage and naturally finds its way to our folk dances as well, but their qualitative contribution at this point is minimal.

As for Solutions

Part of the problem can be solved through workshops, unlike the regular workshops in which only dances for distribution are learned, but rather special workshops designed to enrich the creators among us. I'm sure there will always be room to add knowledge to existing talent. The studied material can shine on the creators' creative work. I think the dance instructors must also participate in these workshops. The connection between creator and instructor is crucial for the joint work.

These classes would not be run by a private entity, for profit, but by a certified body connected to our folk dances that would serve as liaison to the Ministry of Education and receive a special budget for this important purpose. The participants would receive official certification, signed by governmental and professionals, which would grant points to the participant's professional ranking.

We can reach our objective if we manage to hold these classes at least:

a. Twice a year, consistently

b. With maximal participation

c. Treating the matter seriously, as this is our future.

About forty years ago, when I was starting out as a folk dance choreographer, I was already contemplating the idea of including field work in settlements and ethnic communities into the framework of the instructors' training studio's lesson plan, in order to study and document movements and musical material. Unfortunately, the idea fell through, I don't know why. At the time, I did propose to make the instructors' training studios a kind of academy, presenting challenges for every participant and raising the level of the study program with an emphasis on:

a. Choosing candidates to undergo psychological and psychometric exams (the instructor's personality is an important principle with significant influence on the student)

b. Basic classical technique to mold the instructor's personality

c. Expanding the instructor's musical and rhythmic knowledge

d. The pedagogy of instruction

e. Teaching folklore based on elements from ethnic groups living in Israel.

This proposal was also ignored for some reason.

Today we stand before a watering trough that is not just broken but crushed. The Division of Folk Dances and the studios which were the crowning achievement of the Division have ceased to exist.

I'm sure that had we been able to implement these proposals in the past, we wouldn't be facing such a difficult reality today. I must note that the only person who gave any serious thought to my ideas, though she was powerless to help, was Gurit Kadman, the visionary mother of Israeli folk dancing. It was through Gurit Kadman that I discovered my creative skills that brought me this far. It is to her I owe my most heartfelt thanks.

In all honesty I will sum up by saying that art and culture have different ranks of **quality** – Israeli folk dancing should also be treated with respect and not just as a way of letting loose and getting our energies out. If we can only add the necessary **quality** we will all benefit.

The dance held at Beit Danny for my birthday party

f. The Choreographer and the Choreography

(written for a workshop held at the Dancing Conference in Caesarea – January 1995)

In the world of dance, the choreographer is known as a special individual whose ideas, mindset and perspective are different from others. The choreographer breathes life into the bodies of the dancers and the creation, in order to achieve perfection and harmony.

In his choreographical work, the choreographer requires certain qualities and skills, I'll try to expand on them as follows:

1. **Sensitivity:** The great American choreographer **Doris Humphrey** dedicated a few lines in her book **The Art of Making Dance** about the choreographer's sensitivity towards the dancer and placed this virtue above all others. Sensitivity aids the choreographer in understanding the dancer both physically and mentally, allowing maximal use of their potential even before they take the stage.

2. **Imagination:** Imagination aids the choreographer in seeing images, structures and forms before their implementation on stage. A choreographer equipped with a rich imagination can actualize his desires in reality, and the richer and more developed the imagination the more challenging, fascinating and interesting the choreographical work becomes.

3. **Sharp perception:** The eye, one of the most important organs in the human body, has a central and crucial role in our lives – perceiving what happens in our field of vision, providing information to our brains, and like a computer – saving the precise shape in our "memory" and using it when needed. In art in general, and in dance specifically, the eye transmits messages like pleasure, disappointment, boredom and more. If we wish to succeed, the choreographer must be aware and conscious of the laws of the stage, all the parts of its territory, its weaknesses and strengths. Foreknowledge of these subjects will allow correct use of the field and increases the chances of success. The audience watching the troupe's performance also possesses

keen eyes, which makes them the troupe's artistic critic. They come to the show with two possible expectations – enjoyment or disappointment, all determined through the eyes.

4. **Inspiration:** Can an artist without inspiration successfully implement their ideas? Highly doubtful. For the choreographer, inspiration is the motivating and creating force, the "divine spirit", and without it they will experience difficulty in actualizing their creation. Real inspiration expresses the truth and honesty at the core of the artist's soul.

There's no question that without the above properties, the choreographer cannot ascend from amateur work to the level of professionalism. The level of choreography reflects the cultural and spiritual cache in the choreographer's personality, and as wise men have said – a person does not choose their profession, the profession chooses the person.

The Components of a Dance Movement

a. **Structure**

b. **Dynamics**

c. **Rhythm**

d. **Motivation**

a. **Structure:** In choreography, a formal shape without contrasts will be monotonous and uninteresting. In other words, a static ongoing structure on the stage, without change or contrasts in movement, may bore the viewer. American choreographers were the pioneers who created this choreographic style. The phenomenon of contrasts and imbalanced movements is primarily common in modern ballet, which draws interest (this is not the case in the East, with its different culture and traditions of fixed dance styles).

b. **Dynamics:** Daily life is dynamic. What happens around us, the images and experiences that pass before our eyes, the static and the moving figures – all these create an interesting dynamic to which we belong inextricably. The choreographer is tasked with creating this dynamic on the stage. At their disposal are basic movements like sharp, continued, quick, tense and loose, and these must be used as the choreographer sees fit, unlimited in terms of possibilities, with the sole purpose of piquing the viewer's interest.

We are aware of the fact that quick motions agitate while smooth or fluid and slow movements have a calming effect. A good choreographer will never use a single dynamic for extended periods of time, knowing that sharp movements over time may irritate the viewer whereas slow movements over time may put them to sleep. Dynamism is the spice and spine of dance. It's hard to describe a culture without dynamics, without it we would likely die of boredom.

c. **Rhythm:** Of all the components of dance, rhythm has the most influence. Rhythm is one of the exciting foundations of dance. The rhythm is the organizing principle between emphasis and weakening.

Rhythmic forms used properly will grant the dancer and the dance a taste of life. They say that the people who really know what rhythm is, and appreciate it, are tap and jazz dancers. All structures of movement without rhythm endanger the creation, and anyone who lacks a sense of rhythm or whose ability to match sound to physical motion is impaired is a hopeless case. Lacking a sense of rhythm disqualifies a person from working in choreography.

d. **Motivation:** For the dancer, motivation is the ability to convince themselves they can do more, believing that within them lies an energy that can improve their achievements and the quality of their movements. Motivation helps achieve purposes – both personal and collective.

These four elements are the raw material of dance, and without a proper combination of them the dance will be severely lacking. These four must appear to some extent or other in any creation, but it would be better for us to know how to use them in a balanced and informed way, so that all their implications may be understood.

Folk Dancing for the Stage

Folklore is created and evolves in its natural environment alone. Any attempt to implement it in other places and conditions will force us to process this folklore and adjust it to its new environment in order to avoid damaging the product's qualitative value.

The same is true of our folk dances, which also grew and developed under similar circumstances and conditions. They too must undergo the process of adaptation for the stage, which offers us different conditions than those found in their original environment.

I know of a theory that a folk dance performed on the stage must not change its choreographic structure, and the dance must be performed just as it is at least once, from start to finish, before the choreographer makes any necessary changes. Unfortunately, I don't hold with this theory. The stage has its own laws, and without taking these laws into consideration the structure of the dance will be lost.

We must take into account the conditions of a stage surrounded by three walls, with the audience sitting up front and watching, creating conditions which must be addressed, and as a result the dancer must perform their motions in such a way that they are directed towards the audience. For that purpose, we must make the following changes:

1. Planning an entrance onto the stage

2. Planning movement towards the audience

3. Avoiding prolonged movement with our backs to the audience

4. Avoiding repetitive movements (common in folk dances)

5. Finally planning the dancers' exit from the stage.

If we address these five points, we will give the dance an artistic folk aspect, while maintaining what already exists.

Some Ideas for Instructors

1. Keep an ear open for good advice

2. Be true to yourself and don't compromise for the sake of the audience

3. Choose the right music with a dynamic that responds to the needs of your choreographic work

4. Avoid repetition

5. Avoid leaving empty space on the stage. Empty space should be filled with musical interludes or light effects that should take no more than 15-20 seconds at most.

6. When working with short dance pieces, avoid overreliance on the screen or strobing lights. These actions interrupt the continuity and momentum of the piece, preventing it from lifting off the ground and making it difficult for the dancer by demanding further excessive effort to restart the physical

engine again and again, as it dwindles with every stunt relating to lights or the screen.

7. During your work, take time to consider how you would like to conclude the piece you're working on. Don't leave this for a last-minute solution, or you may run out of time and be forced to end the piece with a rashness that may sabotage the entire work.

8. The secret of successful choreographical work lies in flowing and fluid continuity of movement on the stage without pause – surging and calming, aggressive and moderate, light as air and fragile. All these moods create the desired dynamic which, when used properly, will create an enjoyable experience.

I hope the above subjects will serve as cornerstones for instruction and guidance to all those who deal with the subject of ethnic, folk and modern dance, and aid the profession by learning and knowing the subject.

Material gathered and edited by Moshiko, Moshe Yitzhak-Halevy.

A folk dance seminar in Switzerland which I conducted

Appendix One
Travel Journal² in the Land of the Rising Sun³

◎◎◎◎◎◎◎◉◎◉◎◎◎◎◎◎◎

Tuesday, November 20 1979

I'm at the San Francisco airport on my way to Japan, for a series of workshops that will last about five weeks. I've had many dreams in my life and one – visiting the Far East – is coming true before my eyes.

I met Poussey and Hironobu Sanazaki in 1976, at a dance camp in San Diego where I was invited to teach my dances. Fusae and Hironobu had come to the camp from Japan, from one of the suburbs near the city of Tokyo. During one of the days at camp they asked if I'd agree to go on a teaching tour of Japan. The idea appealed to me, but the problem was that we all had very tight schedules. About three years of acquaintance and close contact passed until the right opportunity arrived, and I found myself en route to Japan.

I'd heard much about it, its traditions, its culture and people, their peace and serenity, their dedication and pride as an ancient people.

The loudspeakers announce that passengers of Pan-Am on flight number 11 to Tokyo are now boarding the plane. I am surrounded by Japanese passengers returning to their country, including those who immigrated to America and were taking the opportunity to visit their homeland. A Boeing 747 plane, usually containing over three hundred passengers, is only about a third full. I use this fact to lounge across four seats, trying to use some of the ten-hour flight to sleep.

---

2. The journal is an example of one of many trips I made during my career in Japan and other places in the world.
3. During one of my visits in Japan, I saw a huge sun between the evenings, colored a unique and extraordinary crimson red. I'd never seen the sun at such a size. I couldn't stop looking, and it was then I understood why Japan was called "the Land of the Rising Sun" and why Japan's flag is white with a red sun at its center.

Wednesday, November 21

It's six-thirty in the evening, Japan time, when the long and exhausting flight comes to its end. We land. After border control and customs I find my luggage and make my way out. Poussey and Hironobu are waiting for me here.

The drive from the airport to my hosts' home lasts for nearly three hours, since they moved Tokyo's international airport outside the city. This had infuriated the farming public – rightly concerned that the noise of the airplanes would harm the animals – and caused them to protest against the government. Some of the protests turned violent, and the Japanese government had to turn to the military to suppress them. To this day, more than twenty years later, there is still strict police control, especially for those entering the airport area.

After a warm drink at the home of my hosts and a brief conversation, fatigue has overtaken me and I'm going to bed. Good night, Japan.

Thursday, November 22

The day is dedicated to absolute rest.

Friday, November 23

I woke up early. Today my instructional workshops begin.

This is my first weekend in Japan. The folk-dance organization named "Folk Dance Federation" is the largest organization for folklore in Japan. After driving for an hour and a half down the narrow streets of Tokyo we reached the rendezvous. The heads of the organization welcomed us and the Japanese discipline machine started working. I was given a room where I could set up and organize myself for the workshop. The dancing public began arriving. Only after registration was complete was I asked to take the stage. The sounds of Israeli melodies echoed in the background. Debka Meshuleshet, Ma Navu, Hey Harmonica and more. It seems these were the remnants of Gurit Kadman's last visit to Japan sixteen years ago.

The chairman of the organization began with brief opening remarks, and when he mentioned my name, Moshiko, all the women in the crowd, and the men as well, smiled and even giggled. It turns out that in Japan, most feminine names end with "ko" – Michiko, Taiko and more. To my surprise, I was asked to say a few words. Of course I began by saying how happy I was to be visiting Japan and meeting the Japanese dancing public. I spoke of how Mrs. Gurit Kadman's visit to Japan had greatly benefited Israeli folk dancing, and finally wished us all an enjoyable weekend.

The Japanese Federation asked me to teach the dances collected in my first double album, M.I.H. 1+2. And so in my first workshop I taught Ki Hivshilu, Tfilat HaShachar, HaHelech and Ga'aguim.

Lunch break: a typical Japanese lunch was ordered especially for me: fish soup, fried vegetables, crab legs and rice, and for dessert – Japanese tea and clementines.

The second workshop began at 1:30, with my partner dance – Dror Yikra. I had only managed to teach about two steps when suddenly I was struck by intense pain in my kidneys and back. I couldn't precisely locate the source of these agonizing pains. I could barely stay on my feet. Sweat covered my face and a terrible nausea threatened to tear my breath away. I had to stop the workshop.

After a trip to the bathroom I felt some relief. One of the women, experienced in Japanese massage techniques, offered her assistance. After the treatment I tried to return to the workshop, but not for long, the pains returned and this time they were unbearable. I writhed on the floor, screaming so loud my voice must have reached the heart of heaven itself.

The Japanese organizers decided to call an ambulance. After more than half an hour, the sound of earsplitting sirens heralded its arrival. The ambulance's rocking on the way to the hospital made the pain worse. I had difficulty breathing.

I had never had an experience like this before. It's such a shame it happened far from home, in a foreign environment where I had so much responsibility on my shoulders.

What would happen to my workshops, how would I recover from this problem? I thought along the way. But as I wondered this and tried to find answers we reached the hospital, and wonder of wonders – the pain stopped as if it had never been. The doctor on call examined me and found nothing to justify hospitalization. I felt embarrassed and went back to the theater and the dancing public who awaited me and were pleased to see me return.

It was 3:30. I started organizing the rest of the workshop and was once again struck by agonizing pain. I wept from the pain and events repeated themselves. This time I drove to the hospital in one of the organizers' private vehicles. Chills wracked my whole body as though I had malaria. The doctor suggested keeping me overnight so he could perform some tests the next day and diagnose me.

First my back and waist were X-rayed, then I was moved to an isolated room. There I could scream freely without disturbing other patients.

Along with Poussey, who accompanied me to the hospital, four other men helped hold me down and prevent me from falling off the bed due to my pain-induced writhing. I begged Poussey to get the doctor to inject me with a sedative. The doctor came with a small needle bearing a small amount of medicine, injecting it into my shoulder muscle. It was about as helpful as cupping on a corpse, the pain continued. I asked Poussey to bring him back, and this time begged and pleaded with him to inject the sedative directly into the vein in my arm. After he did so I felt a relief and ease that allowed me to get some sleep.

At eleven at night I woke up as if nothing had happened. I wanted to leave the hospital, but had to wait until 9:30 the next morning, when the doctors began their shift.

Saturday, November 24

The specialist doctor decided there was no point in keeping me at the hospital. He prescribed some medication for me and after Poussey paid the 120-dollar fee for the night I'd stayed at the hospital, I was released. The hospital had in fact demanded 200 dollars, but I insisted the price was irrational and received an 80-dollar discount – what's wrong with that?

I left the hospital on my way to the group of dancers waiting for me. After a two-hour drive we reached the rendezvous. At 1:30 in the afternoon I arrived to pick up where we'd left off the day before. The dancers were happy to see me after witnessing what I'd been through. I was warmly received with thunderous applause. I went to work with considerable hesitation for fear the pain might return. I managed to teach four dances: Mishal, Hora Chemed, Debka Bedouit, and Ga'aguim by special request.

At 5 PM we went to dinner. It was the same meal I'd received the day before. I developed anxieties and sensitivities to Japanese food. The smell of the stews made my stomach flutter with nausea.

At 6 PM we returned to the theater. The dancers repeated the dances they'd learned. At 6:30 I gave another class to replace the one I was meant to teach that morning. I managed to teach two more dances: Et Dodim Kala and Debka Kurdit.

The Japanese were thrilled with the Kurdish debka. We repeated all the dances they had learned so far.

Time flew by and we had to leave the theater before 9 PM, when the outer gate was automatically closed by order of the government. Feeling good, I returned to my hosts' house. Fatigue helped me fall asleep quickly.

Sunday, November 25

At 9 AM the class began. I worked with the same group of dancers and presented the movie "Come, Yemen" – the creation of Gurit Kadman, a copy of which I'd acquired from the Department of Folk Dances. After the screening, I took questions. At 10 we resumed dancing. I taught HaMecholelet and Debka Uriya, the latter of which was received with great success.

At 12:00 there was a lunch break, and at 1:00 we returned to the theater for a general review of all the material. At 2:30 we stopped dancing. The head of the Federation asked everyone to gather around for a closing ceremony.

Suddenly the dancers formed two groups – men on the right and women on the left – with a group of men appearing between the two, apparently Federation members and another group of dignitaries related to the organizing committee. After a speech by the Chairman and some members of the Committee, the dancers returned to the floor for a final dance. They asked to close the day out with Debka Uriya, and returned to the group format.

Then I was asked to say a few words, through my hostess Poussey who was translating to Japanese. I said I'd heard of the quality of the Japanese dancing public from a few colleagues, but I could not have imagined the extent to which reality outshone any description. "Usually," I said, "I carry with me memories and experiences from my work around the world, this visit in Japan and meeting the dancers will be another precious link in the chain of my memories. There is no doubt," I added, "that this visit will be an important chapter in my book that will be published someday. I hope and wish that the understanding and happiness between the dancers will spread into a global movement. I will not say goodbye, but until next time, and thank you!"

The applause was encouraging and the crowd began to disperse. Many found their way to me – some for photos, some for autographs on the records or shirts they'd purchased, and some just to shake hands. You don't normally see handshakes in Japan, as is customary in other parts in the world, as in Japan everything is done through bows at a certain distance. Many of the dancers escorted me all the way to the car that drove me to my hosts' house. I felt that same public, so restrained during the lessons, had freed themselves from traditional habits to express themselves warmly and openly to me.

My first week in Japan concluded successfully. I thank God I was able to physically withstand the task. After a hot Japanese shower I stayed up to write these lines. Then I went to bed for a good night's sleep.

Monday, November 26

I woke up at 11 AM and the plan was to go out into the center of Tokyo, a 40-minute ride by train. The purpose of the trip was to deliver film rolls for development, but it turned out they had to send the film to the United States. I gave up on the idea and decided to wait until I returned to New York.

At 3:30 in the afternoon I was invited to the Israeli Consulate, to meet Mr. **Azriel Galon**, advisor to the Ambassador, who also happened to be of Yemenite descent. During the meeting we had an interesting conversation about folklore and folk dancing, but I was forced to cut the discussion short due to a relapse of pain in my back and kidneys. I excused myself and planned to leave before the pain increased. I received two capsules of aspirin to soothe the pain, but they failed. On our way to the train station we stopped at a pharmacy to buy some kind of pain medication, but it didn't help either.

The train ride to my hosts' home was unbearable. I had to go the whole way standing up, horribly crowded. Unfortunately, the Japanese have no sentimentality towards the elderly, pregnant women or parents with babies. Mostly they're ignored, even by young men and students. The phrase "respect your elders" is unknown in their provinces. My pain and suffering didn't matter to anyone in the slightest. I thought I would go mad.

When we disembarked at the station I couldn't continue walking. We took a cab and quickly reached my hosts' house. I fell on the mattress (no beds) and sobbed in agony, the pain in my back and stomach was awful.

There was no other recourse but to call a doctor, but to my great surprise doctors don't make house calls in Japan; if someone has a problem they have to go to the hospital themselves, and so I too was forced to drive there. The doctor at the hospital explained that I was suffering from an intestinal virus that was, at the time, common across all of Japan. Indeed, the medicine I received alleviated the pain in my stomach and back. I made it through the night "with awe and reverence", praying to God to make me well as soon as possible and restore me to myself, so I could complete my obligations in Japan.

Tuesday, November 27

I tried to stay in bed as much as possible. A general weakness and a sense of instability in my stomach continued to haunt me. I had difficulty eating. No food could remain in my belly. I tried an Israeli American breakfast – two poached eggs, warm milk, toast with jam. I ate without appetite, just to have something in me in case I had to purge again.

I had to make my way by train again to a class that was booked for that evening. In light of my overall state I thought it would be better to take a car, but such a trip would take twice as long due to the heavy traffic on the streets of Japan. The Japanese prefer public transportation as well.

After a forty-five-minute journey on the train we had to meet the young Japanese woman who had organized the evening at the station. Even before disembarking I started to feel pain. I was worried I might have to cancel the class. I took some pills I'd brought with me and felt better. We were still early, and entered a café to drink something warm. While the pain had diminished, the sense of nausea constantly accompanied me. Now we had to take a cab for twenty minutes to the meeting place.

There was a chill in the theater. All the participants were bundled up in scarves, sweaters and coats to preserve their body heat. I was surprised they were willing to hold the activity in an unheated theater, being at the end of the cold month of November. But despite the intense cold, the reception was warm, like everywhere else I'd been. I was introduced to the person in charge of the place, and the President and Vice-President. This order exists almost everywhere in Japan – the person responsible for the seminar opens the event and the President and Vice-President close it. I taught Yankale Levy's Ki Eshmera, Chiribim,

Neima Tajikit and Yankale Levy's Bat Teiman.

During the break traditional Japanese tea was served, which I shared with the President, the Vice President, the organizer and Poussey. We had some light conversation and I went back to work.

At the end of the evening, after the organizers offered their thanks, there was a warm round of applause, and as usual – shaking hands, autographing records and shirts.

Fortunately, one of the participants named **Korosawa** offered to drive us home. I lay in the backseat the entire ride – I felt unwell and weak. At my hosts' home I went to bed and fell asleep. Another day had passed.

Wednesday, November 28

My class today was an all-female group of high school students studying Sports and Folk Dances. On arriving at the school one of the older students invited me to a brief conversation in the principal's office. She had apparently taken one of my workshops in the past, and she was the one who had recommended that the principal invite me.

Teaching a workshop in Japan

The custom in Japan is to remove your shoes at the entrance to homes and theaters. 300 pairs of shoes – the number of participating students – had been placed on the stairwell. The students were herded into the theater dressed stylishly, not traditionally Japanese but in a variety of outfits from all over the world.

I was greeted with applause. I felt the warmth and encouragement I needed in light of my medical condition. I told myself I would do whatever it took to succeed, so that the public here left the class with great satisfaction. I prayed it would be so.

Before starting the class, two groups of students put on a demonstration for me – one danced an Italian-style tarantella while another performed a Balkan dance. The level of the performances was exceptional. In light of the many participants I asked Poussey to arrange the girls in a circle.

The message was quickly received, and before I could say "Jack Robinson" the girls had formed six circles, remarkably ordered and without running. Each of the students took a step or two to join the circle closest to her. I was astonished by the order and discipline. When I wanted to demonstrate a certain move, the two circles nearest to the center would naturally sit on the floor, the third and fourth circles knelt down, and the fifth and sixth circles stood. It was all done in exemplary silence. What a pleasure!

I'd already met with large groups before. The largest had been 250 people, but the difference was that everywhere else I'd had to insist on discipline and quiet during the lesson, whereas here in Japan there was no need to even mention the subject. Half the students were having their first experience with folklore, but with the concentration skills typical of them they executed the movements as though they were practically professionals. I enjoyed this meeting and will surely remember it for years to come.

The class began with twenty minutes of warm-ups and practice, based on Yemenite elements and others that exist in Israeli folk dance, and then came the dances: Se'i Yona, Ki Eshmera, Bat Teiman, all by Yankale Levy. His dances aided me whenever I met groups of dancers who lacked prior experience. Many of his dances excelled in style, grace and beauty, and were popular around the world.

My meeting with the high school students was among the most successful

I'd had in Japan. At its end I was given a gift on behalf of the school – an artistically-designed Japanese doll. I finished the successful class with words of gratitude and the hope that I would see them again.

After the class we went to the guest room, where I was offered a light drink and cake, and after a brief conversation we parted ways with the possibility that I'd be invited again to give a longer class, a seminar that would last several days. The idea appealed to me.

On our way back to my hosts' house we stopped at a restaurant to have dinner. I felt my health slowly recovering and went to bed tired but satisfied.

Thursday, November 29

I woke up relatively early. This time I wanted to buy a camera. We took the train into town, standing for more than half an hour. The heat and density created a bottleneck, but ultimately we reached our intended destination. Here as well, at the Yoto-Bashi-Camera store, there were many customers. The store was considered one of the largest for photography purposes. I purchased a professional "Bronica" camera for portrait shots. We had dinner in town, and at home I perused the camera's manual. I was very pleased with my purchase. It was late, I was dying to get some sleep.

At a train station in Japan

Friday, November 30

The class was planned to start at 1:30 in the afternoon. We had to take an early train. We reached our destination at noon. The two women who had organized the meeting were already waiting for us at the station and took us to a nearby restaurant to warm our hearts with a good meal.

The class was meant for a group of sixty women, housewives taking one day a week off from their housework to learn dance. I very much enjoyed teaching them to dance. Their level was quite good. I taught them Se'i Yona by Yankale Levy in couples, Oy Yossel Yossel and Daasa. From there we continued on to the distant city of Kyoto. We hitched a ride for an hour and a half to the central train station, and from there we took a bullet train for another three hours. The train ride was pleasant and quiet. Japanese trains are considered the fastest in the world.

At 10 PM we reached Kyoto, and from the station we took a cab to the hotel. We placed our luggage in our rooms and immediately went out into the street to take in the city's atmosphere, but it was so late there wasn't much to see – everything was closed. We returned to the hotel at 2 AM. After a full day of teaching and taking the train I swiftly fell asleep.

Saturday, December 1

We took advantage of the morning hours to briefly stroll down a street that primarily consisted of food stores. We had to make our way through the crowd that had gone out shopping. An abundance of products was on display. I think the Japanese mainly subsist on seafood, like varieties of fish, but on fried vegetables as well, and let us not forget the traditional rice which is their basic food, like bread is to us. The Japanese love eating rice in its natural flavor, but every now and then they spice it up with sauces. The strong scents of stews overwhelmed our breath.

We had to make our way back to the hotel in order to meet the organizers of the five-day workshop in Kyoto that had been arranged for me. I was informed that the group had already been active for a year and its members loved Israeli dances, to the point of dancing them exclusively and showing an interest in Israel's current affairs.

After a brief meeting with the organizers we drove for over half an hour to the workshop's location. The house, which was also a boarding house, hosted various cultural activities and had rooms to let. I managed to grab a quick snack before starting the class.

It's 2 PM. About sixty men and women came to the class. Usually the group consists of twenty people, but the event had drawn in participants from more distant places as well. In the first part of the class I taught Tama Temima, VeSamachta BeHageicha and Ya Abud.

The level of the dancers' skill surprised me. I was amazed by how quickly they learned, and their quiet discipline. My every comment was received with a bow and the word "Hai!", meaning that my words were understood. And reader, do not think these were professional dancers. Their concentration and ability to translate everything to action were truly amazing. Usually I teach three dances per class, but here in Japan I had managed to teach five or six. Much respect to the Japanese dancers!

Wandering the shops of Japan

We have taken a dinner break. I was given a typical Japanese room at the boarding house, without a bed or furniture, just a small table with the traditional teapot and beautifully drawn cups for self-service, a phone for internal communication and a TV that worked on hundred-yen coins for one hour at a time. On the floor mat a thin mattress had been spread out, with a thick warm blanket and a relatively small pillow filled with rice grains. Anyone unused to this would probably feel uncomfortable, but when fatigue falls upon you you're less picky and get used to this as well. The surrounding silence and the clean sheets helped me take a 45-minute nap until my second class began at 6:30 in the evening. Working in Japan taught me that rest is better than wasting time in restaurants. My hosts always made sure I had plenty of sandwiches and drinks. During my second lesson I taught Zachariah, Ya Habib, Hora Yamit and Yelalat HaRuach.

Every single dance was greeted with excitement, and not just out of politeness. The dancers didn't rest for a moment. Even when I called a break they took advantage of it to write the dances down and repeat the ones they'd learned. I couldn't help but be impressed at their attitude and how seriously they took the dances. There was no point in asking them to repeat the movements, and all I had to do was teach them new ones, which I did quite gladly.

The class ended with an exceptional atmosphere. The dancers drifted apart – some to rest, some to converse and some to sleep – to gather strength for the following day. As is my habit, I sat down to write these lines until my eyes closed.

Sunday, December 2

At 9:30 AM, after breakfast, the class began. I taught BeTof UTzlil, Eshal Elohai, Bat Teiman by Yankale Levy and HaMavdil.

It was clear that the Japanese dancers were very fond of Yemenite dances. Their small bodies were a perfect fit for Yemenite movements, many of them moved as though they were Yemenites themselves, all that was missing were the costumes. After lunch, at 1:30, my last class of the weekend began. The plan was to review all the dances I'd taught in the last two days. We were done with all the material within half an hour, leaving me no choice but to teach two more dances: Chiribim and Yaffo. The two dances were received quite well and the weekend ended with a wonderful feeling. We parted ways after taking photos together, signing records, handing out shirts and exchanging various pieces of paper.

On Monday and Tuesday evenings I had more classes in that same theater, and many of the participants promised to return. I gave warm handshakes to those who lived far away and couldn't participate, hoping we would meet again someday.

Monday, December 3

My hosts and I took advantage of the morning hours to tour the outskirts of Kyoto, which according to Japanese history was the nation's capital until a little more than a century ago. The city held historical ruins which served as tourist attractions for visitors, with a special street of geishas that had existed for many years. The geishas were not cheap women, but women educated and trained to serve as hostesses. Each was an artist in her own right, some playing instruments and singing wonderfully, some serving tea in traditional Japanese ceremonies. Visiting a geisha is a very expensive service. Only wealthy men with financial means can afford such a luxury. Every geisha has her men and she does not accept anyone without reliable recommendations. I saw a few of them – each beautiful, tastefully dressed and walking down the street with grace and elegance.

The day passed quickly and we returned to the hotel to rest, then have some dinner and get to work. A cab drove us there. I had to start at 7:00.

The familiar sounds of dances taught over the weekend greeted us. New and familiar faces in the theater. I was greeted warmly. Tonight I taught Al Yadil, Se'i Yona in couples by Yankale Levy, Marhaba and my own variation on Se'i Yona in a circle.

After the class we got a ride back to the hotel. We placed our belongings in our rooms and went out looking for an open restaurant. The weather was pleasant during our stay in Kyoto, though in the evenings it did get a little colder. How pleasant it was to return to the warm room at the hotel. Another day passed.

Tuesday, December 4

Today we once again toured the outskirts of the city. I bought two watches I liked, and after a three-hour walk we returned to the hotel to rest up for the class. In the evening I taught Oy Yossel Yossel, Hey Yo Ya and Eliyahu Gamliel's Dror Yikra.

After the class the entire group invited me to a café that was also a restaurant, and held a humble ceremony where they gifted me with a souvenir – a flag with the stitched portrait of one of their temples.

At the end of the evening I parted ways with Kyoto's dancing public – a small yet warm and kindhearted public. We returned to the hotel. This time I decided to stay in and concentrate on preparations for my return to Tokyo the next day.

Wednesday, December 5

I got up at 9:15 – a hot shower and shave refreshed my body. Our train left at 1:15 – an express train to Tokyo, with reserved seats for us.

There were guiding arrows drawn on the platforms indicating to the public where they should stand in line and where the train doors open, which prevents unnecessary running around on the platform. A foreigner in this country encountering these phenomena couldn't help but be impressed and amazed at all the things that might appear meaningless, but spare the public considerable bother.

Two minutes before the train left, we suddenly saw the manager of Kyoto's dance group coming to say goodbye. We didn't manage to say much beyond waving through the window. The train left the platform exactly on time.

After three hours we had nearly reached tumultuous Tokyo, and again switched to a local train that would take us to my hosts' house.

We made it in good time. I did my laundry, made a few phone calls, had dinner, sat down to write these lines and went to bed.

Thursday, December 6

I woke up at 11:00 after an excellent night's sleep.

The plan was to go to the bank and transfer money to my account in New York and prepare for my class in Tokyo. I managed to rest a bit before leaving. We had to leave early to make sure we'd make it on time.

I'd already mentioned the tumultuous traffic in the narrow streets of Tokyo in a previous entry. We reached the place at 6:30 and saw the dancing group warming up. It was the cold month of December and most of the theaters weren't heated.

After the opening ceremony and a few words I said to the dancing public and my hosts, I began the class. I taught dances in this order: Ya Abud, Yelalat HaRuach, BeTof UTzlil, Marhaba and Tama Temima.

Five dances were an unusual pace for two hours of instruction. I'd already noted I can usually only teach three to four dances in that time anywhere in the world, but here in Japan I can do so much more.

The records I'd brought with me to sell in Japan had almost run out as well. I'd sold 150 double albums of MIH 1-2, 81 of MIH 3, 75 of MIH 4 and another 75 of MIH 5.

There was a demand for more records and I still had a substantial number of classes left. I decided to make a list of interested people, and I would send the required amount when I returned to New York. After the class, we stopped at one of the restaurants for dinner. The custom was to eat after class, not before. After the meal we went straight home, ran some errands and prepared for an early rise the next day. I went to bed at midnight.

Friday, December 7

Woke up at 5 AM. At 6:15 we were already in the car. We left early to avoid traffic jams, considering we had a five-hour drive ahead of us. We were going away to a weekend series of classes, Friday through Sunday. After a long and excruciating drive we finally reached a small and pleasant boarding house. I had about two and a half hours before my first class, which I used to get some sleep.

At 2:15 I was awakened to prepare for the class. The number of participants wasn't high, there is still little awareness of Israeli dances in Japan. Many of the

Japanese dancers look down on Israeli folk dances and prefer Balkan dances from Yugoslavia, Macedonia, Romania, Bulgaria, Turkey, Armenia, Greece and more, which they dance with great passion. But the ones who did come to my workshops out of curiosity found that my dances were just as challenging.

When I first came to Japan it seemed that many of the dancers I brought with me danced in the style of Mayim Mayim, Hora Medura and more from the same category. For Israelis, these dances are an undeniable asset and part of the historical development of Israeli folk dance in Israel, but for the Japanese dancer seeking challenges, the dances I've named hold no appeal at all.

However, during my stay in Japan a rumor spread that the dances I taught were different from what was expected. Some of the dancers were the curious type coming to examine me and my dances up close, while the rest were familiar faces from previous meetings all over Japan. I was introduced to the group, and after opening remarks from Poussey the organizer, I began teaching Shma Ha'El, Uri Tzafon and Yaffo.

The skills of these participants were much higher than any other group I'd taught in Japan. The first two dances were quickly picked up, despite their unique Yemenite style. I had to think of other dances from my repertoire. Fortunately, I have quite a lot of material that could challenge them. In the evening I was free but wanted to observe from the sidelines and enjoy this excellent group of dancers.

Saturday, December 8

Even before opening my eyes, breakfast in my room was already prepared. What service! It was 9:15, and the class began at 9:30, but there was no reason to worry – I made it on time and taught HaHelech in lines, Machol HaShnaim in couples, El HaAyin in a circle and Kissufim in couples.

The class was pleasant. The Japanese dancers are much better at line and circle dances, but in couples they have a bit of a problem – it's difficult for them to relate to each other during the dance. The reason stems from ancient Japanese tradition. They are an internalized and introverted people. A boy could run to the partner with whom he wishes to dance and vice versa, but during the dance it is difficult for them to look in each other's eyes. They look away and only steal glances at each other.

I think I was the first person to teach couple dances in Japan. No one had said anything to me personally about it, or prepared me in advance for the fact that this was not a popular form of dance in Japan. Regardless, it was not my intent to change centuries-old traditions and habits, and yet I still feel that over time progress will overcome tradition in various fields, and dance will do its part to bring about this change. After the class we went out to lunch and then to rest.

At 2:30 the second class began, in which I taught Debka Raffiyach in lines, Alei Giva in couples, HaMangina Sheli in couples and Debka Knaan in lines. We took a dinner break and at 7:00 everyone was already back in the theater for freestyle dancing and a review of the material we'd covered during the day. The Japanese dancers usually do this without my help. I only observe from the sidelines and make comments when necessary.

At 9 PM the dance ended. I stayed behind to videotape their dances. I wanted precise and accurately documented material to study when needed.

A few days later I returned to New York.

After the seminar in Japan, pictures taken with the dancers

Appendix Two
Poems

Awaken You Sleepers — 8.10.2000 (following events in the Territories)

Awaken you sleepers, open your eyes
Do not sink into the sleep of illusions.
Wake up, sleepers, bend your ears
and hear the bullets whistling.

The echoes of the drums of war are upon us
Pounding on our doors.
And our neighbors from the Fatach
turn their weapons on us.

Awaken you sleepers, the land is burning.
We are at war, the government says,
Now is the time to join together
for we have no other choice.

The dove of peace has changed its feathers,
its face revealed as that of an eagle.
Cruelly its eyes narrow
to sink its talons in our flesh.

How long will we fool ourselves
and walk in this empty, blasted space.
The time has come to plant our feet
on the ground and wake up.

Strange Morning – 25.8.98

This morning I woke up and you weren't beside me
your embracing hand did not rest on my body
Where did you disappear to so suddenly
while I naively stayed asleep?

You left the window of my room open
and the pages of my poems fluttered in the wind
The morning chill penetrated my body
and raindrops tapped on my roof.

Your behavior is wrapped in mystery
No words and no explanations
Should I wait, should I hope,
you might return after all?

If you decide to return to the nest of my love,
For you I will conquer my feelings of pride.
Just please don't forget,
lock my door when you come home.

The Dream – 20.6.98

As I sleep I always dream
of flying and floating in the air,
executing hair-raising tricks
and again awaiting the audience's applause.

I turn right and return to the left,
hovering in the air like a great vulture,
diving down and kissing the ground,
lifting my head and disappearing into space.

The view from above is beautiful and thrilling
and everyone down there stares and wonders,
how does he do it? they ask,
and, satisfied, I continue my stunts.

There is no magic, no miracle here
Just imagination in a variety of colors.
Anyone who wants to feel like me,
must dream my dreams at night.

The Magic of the Smile – 29.8.98

If you were born with a smile on your lips
Know how blessed by fate you are
it will add grace to your features
and charm to your personality.

It has the power to impress those near and far
Make companions and friends
Melt hearts, conquer loves
and pave the way to great success.

But you must remember
to use your smile wisely,
smartly, thoughtfully, intelligently.
If the smile can grant some happiness
Do so with joy and honesty and integrity.

Because the smile on your face
is not your personal property
but entrusted to you
to share with others
like any gift from God.

Remember, Girl – 3.2.1998

Words and Melody: Moshe Yitzhak-HaLevy (Moshiko)

Remember, girl
the birthdays
we played together
by the strawberry tree
and from time to time
we also reached out,
plucking strawberries
Fistfuls at a time.
We climbed, we jumped
in the great field.
All around was green
drowning in sand.
And in the evening…
On cold days
We lit fires,
and sang songs.

And deep in the night
When the fire went out
the darkness enveloped
every bush and tree.
And we parted
without saying a word
with a touch of comfort
for the wonderful day.

Years have passed
you are now a woman
you do not play
you are more sensitive.
The strawberry tree is gone too
You can't see the field anymore
Just houses and houses
And a Beit Midrash beside them.
Where are you today
and what are you doing?
Are you happy
to be a woman?
And what about a husband,
are there children?
You're drowning in joy,
They must be cute.

I was just remembering
those days
when we two
were children.
I've been a father for years
I have children too,
I'm a grandfather too now
Surrounded by grandchildren.

On Love – 18.10.2004

So much has been written
on love
how thrilling it is, how exalted
And yet it is not common to all
and only a few experience it

Love has so many faces
There is free love
and forbidden love
Open and concealed
Sweet and bitter
and there are those
who will take risks for it

It infiltrates the nobility
Dressed in lace and chiffon
Descending to the people
like the whisper of the ocean waves
Thirsting for life in the darkness
Ruling us with a strong hand

That's what love is
Invasive and tempestuous
And all who've tasted it
know… it is as essential as breath.

The Right to Live – 24.4.98

A.

What more must man do
to be granted the right to live?
How do we stay sane,
without a sense of body and a groaning soul?

B.

Because he no longer resembles a human,
skin wrinkled down to his bones,
mouth agape, voiceless,
choked with tears.

C.

On bright days he is all yearning
and on dark days he will long for hope
and in heavy rains he will pray
for God to come quickly.

D.

But the day is late in coming, from where will it arrive
and where is God hiding in the heavens?
His voice is no longer heard
and to whom would he turn for salvation?

E.

If God will come tomorrow
Perhaps it will be too late
Because he no longer has the strength to wait
He has lost the hope of living on.

The Truth and the Heart – April 1998

The Truth	The Heart
a. Each of us has a moment of truth which we are forced to confront.	Each of us has a heart beating strong with a thousand rooms of storage.
b. You alone and with no one else must find the answers, and not renounce them.	Love, hatred, jealousy, friendship, grief and joy, smiles and sadness.
c. Because the truth has many faces, some beautiful some evil	Vanity and humility, foolishness and cleverness, hopes, disappointments, softness and wickedness.
d. They are part of you Do not ignore them, From them you cannot escape.	Time is short to contain the reasons that dwell in our hearts and do not wear down.
e. So stand with pride, my friend Do not despair You will prevail	From time to time they'll rise up breathe in deep and trouble us.
f. Because it is your truth alone that stays with you for all time.	That is what our hearts are Small and delicate Commanding us to accept their judgments.

Appendix Three
Moshe Yitzhak-HaLevy Biography

Moshe Yitzhak-Halevy, known to the dancing public worldwide as Moshiko Halevy, was born in 1932 in the Manshiya area near Kerem HaTeimanim, to Yemenite immigrants.

At seventeen he encountered the world of dance at Mia Arbatova's ballet school. After three months of training Moshiko was asked to join Mia Arbatova's ballet troupe, in which he successfully performed as a character dancer.

The critical public noticed his apparent talent, despite the small roles he played, a mere three months after he'd started dancing.

Moshiko dedicated his first years as a dancer to classical ballet techniques, which to him constituted the basis for all the other dance styles he would engage with: modern ballet, jazz, tap, and various character dances.

Moshiko completed his military service in the military band – with "HaKarmel" for the first six months and then in the "Dance Squadron".

With his discharge Moshiko joined the Li La Lo and Do Re Mi theaters, in which he appeared as a dancer in musical plays. He was also invited to dance in the troupe of dancer and choreographer Naomi Aleskovsky, replacing Yonatan Karmon who retired.

In 1953 Moshiko joined the Inbal dance troupe, on the recommendation of renowned choreographer Jerome Robbins who was staying in Israel and giving a special class on dance in the field of classical-modern ballet for select dancers, in which Moshiko HaLevy also participated. In Inbal Moshiko served as one of its primary dancers, and in 1957 he joined the troupe on a tour of Europe and the United States.

In 1959, during his time with Inbal, Moshiko created his first dance, Debka Uriya, which won the silver medal in the Dance Festival held in Vienna, Austria. It later became one of the most popular dances in Israeli folk dance classes, and a challenge for every representational dance troupe.

In 1962, with his return to Israel after Inbal's second tour in the United States, Moshiko left Inbal and joined dancer Yona Levy and musician Itzhak Eliezerov to found the HaPaamonim troupe, which achieved great success in Israel and abroad. As the artistic director and choreographer, Moshiko focused his choreographical works on the subject of the ethnic folklore of the various cultures in Israel, and on artistically adapting them to the needs of the stage.

While working with his troupe Moshiko was invited by the Arab Department of the Histadrut HaKlalit to serve as artistic director and instructor for minority troupes – Cherkasies from Kfar Kama in the Galil, Druze from the village of Osafiya in the Carmel and Arabs from the village of Tira in the Triangle. Later Moshiko gave instruction in the village of Taibe in the Triangle region on behalf of Reshet Amal. For the five years he fulfilled this function, Moshiko established the troupes, guided them, and built them a performance repertoire with the crown jewel being the participation of the Osafiya and Kfar Kama troupes in the Dance Festival in Holland and Belgium, and winning awards and acclaim.

In 1969 Moshiko was invited to the Wingate Institute to establish a representational dance troupe along with teacher Nina Orad z"l as a choreographer and artistic director, and even toured with them throughout Germany. In 1971, after ten years of independent activity, Moshiko was asked to return to the Inbal theater, this time as the troupe manager. During his time as troupe manager Moshiko was asked by Sara Levy-Tanai to prepare two choreographies – one, an original Yemenite dance for men, and the other a Chabani dance – for a program consisting of short sections called miniatures. Both dances earned the theater's Cameri program great success for 12 years.

In 1973, on the second day of the Yom Kippur War, Moshiko again departed with the troupe for a two-month tour in the United States. At the end of the tour, Moshiko concluded his obligations to the theater and stayed in America to work independently. He also expanded his field of work to include Europe, the Far East and Israel.

While staying in America Moshiko was invited to prepare two choreographical pieces for a pair of modern dance troupes from Canada – one in Ottawa and the other in Toronto. Moshiko received positive feedback from the cultural critics of Ottawa and Toronto.

In 2008 Moshiko decided to open his own dance class at Beit Dani, along with the dance instructor Haim Tzemach. Today Moshiko's classes include dance instructors such as Eyal Krablink, Tamir Shalev, Michal Bachar and other dance instructors willing to contribute their experience to this evening. At the event Moshiko's dances are taught and performed, along with the dances of other instructors.

From 1949 to today Moshiko HaLevy has spent 67 active years in the field of dance, 57 of which involved creating approximately 300 Israeli folk dances. Moshiko has also composed over 200 melodies to accompany his dances. Moshiko also wrote lyrics to some of his melodies. At present Moshiko has produced eighteen records, and published the "Kachol Lavan" notebook for instructors traveling abroad. This notebook has been of great service to Israeli dance instructors invited to teach abroad.

Moshiko's dances are performed and requested all over the world, and he is frequently invited to teach workshops and seminars at dance camps for the dancing public in America, Russia, England, France, Holland, Switzerland, Germany, the Czech Republic and Belgium, New Zealand, Australia, Japan, Hong Kong and Taiwan.

Dancing at an Israeli folk dance seminar in California

Pictures from My Life

My Family

With my wife Michal

With my daughter Yochemed

With my wife and children Ben-Ya and Libi

With my children Yiftach, Chamad and Oria

Yona Levy, Itzik Eliezerov and my son Ben-Ya

With my children Ben-Ya and Libi

With my sister Bracha

Nostalgia

Presenting Shirat Dvora at the Har-Tuv Institute

The soccer team of the Har-Tuv Institute children

On Yama Beach in Israel

In my youth

A dancer in Mia Arbatova's studio

With opera singer Mordechai Ben-Shachar and HaBima actor Avraham Ronai

At a tap-dancing performance

On one of my trips to the airport

With the HaPaamonim troupe touring abroad

From the play Mischak HaPijama, in a Spanish dance

Promotional photo of HaPaamonim

With Gabi Amrani on the roof of my house in Kerem HaTeimanim

At Piccadilly Square in London

A Chinese painter from Hong Kong with my portrait

Folk Dance Camps

San Diego Camp, California 1976

San Diego Camp, California 1989

The teaching team for Camp Hora Shalom in America

All the participants of Camp Hora Shalom

Camp Hora Shalom, America

Instruction team at a weekend in Lille, France

My folk-dance seminar in Hong Kong

With groups of dancers in Hong Kong

A folk dance group from Hong Kong which I instructed

With friends from Hong Kong, members of the Bublet ballet organization

A family of dancers in Hokkaido, Japan, and my manager Poussey, first on the left

With Friends and Colleagues

With Felix Fibish, Jewish dance artist

Yemenite dance with Yudaleh Cohen

With Reuven Stern, Michai David and Israel Yakovee in Los Angeles

A conversation with Raffi Damar

With Uziel z"l, a Chesed dancer

With Yankale Levy

With Moshe Telem

With Yossi the accordionist, Meir Shem-Tov, Shmulik Gov-Ari and Moshe Telem

רגעים - אלכם הובר 0523366940

With Moshe Telem and Shlomo Maman

With Shlomo Maman and my grandson Michael

With Yedid Meir Ovadia and Itzchak Eliezerav

A hug from Yudaleh Cohen on my birthday

With Avner Naim, Reshet Gimel broadcaster

With Moti Alfasi z"l

With the creator and chairman of the Dance Instructors' and Creators' Organization Ilan Swissa and choreographer Yoram Sasson

Me with Eliyahu Gamliel

With Tirtza Hodes

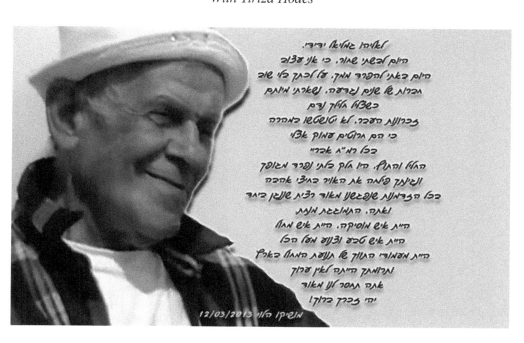

Press and Documentation

MOSHIKO
...giving folk dance lessons

כחול לבן

התנהגות אישית

יש לזכור, כי להתנהגות אישית נאותה של המדריך
הן במסגרת עבודתו, והן מחוצה לה נודעת חשיבות
רבה והיא מהווה מופת לציבור הרוקדים.
כמדריך עליך לדעת, שעבודתך אינה מתמקדת
בהדרכה בלבד. נוכחותך באירועים שונים הקשורים
בעיקר בהשתלמות במחנה, הינה חשובה ביותר.
המדובר הוא בפעילויות שתוכנן הוא הווי
ושמטרתן ליצור מצב רוח טוב ואווירה נעימה.
אם אתה המדריך גם בעל כישורים בתחום הזמר,
נגינה או תיפוף, תהיה תרומתך לאווירה הכללית
משמעותית ביותר וציבור הרוקדים ידע להעריך זאת
היטב.

הערה: לצערי, יש לנו מחסור במדריכים בעלי כישורים
בתחום הבידור במיוחד באותם נושאים שהזכרתי
לעיל.

כחול לבן

כן יש לקחת בחשבון חשיבות הופעתו האסתטית של
המדריך, בפני ציבור הרוקדים. וכאן ההזדמנות להציע
לך המדריך רשימת ביגוד למען הרגשתך הטובה.

1. שנים שלושה זוגות מכנסים בסיגנון טריינינג.
2. מס' סביר של חולצות טריקו.
3. ארבעה עד חמישה זוגות גרביים.
4. נעלי התעמלות נוחות ללא זיזים בולטים בסוליה.
   על הסוליה להיות חלקה על כדי למנוע היצמדות
   יתר של הסוליה לרצפה, שבעקבותיה מופיעים
   כאבי ברכיים לא נעימים. כדאי לקחת זוג נוסף של
   נעלי ג'אז עם סוליית דקות מעור, המתאימות לכל
   רצפה בעלת תחושה דביקה.
5. ואף זאת : ואל תראה בכך דבר טפל : עליך המדריך
   להצטייד במספר מגבות קטנות, שהן מאד חיוניות
   לכל מדריך המזיע בעבודתו.
6. ואחרון חביב וחשוב. עליך להצטייד בדיאודורנט
   ריחני לגוף. זהו ללא ספק פריט חיוני לכל מדריך
   בפעולה.

חולית המחול הצבאית

חברי הלהקה: ניסן יתיר, תמר זברוצקי, לילי ולקובסקי ולילי בן יוסף, משה לזרע ומשה לוי
והאקורדיוניסט ניסימזוב

גלגולים רבים עברו על להקות הצבאיות. החל
ב„ציזבטרון", וכלה בלהקת „איילון", שאנשיהם סיימו
את שירותם בצבא והתפזרו מי לביתו, מי ל„הבימה",
ל„קאמרי", ל„המטאטא" ועוד.

עתה קיימת בצבא שתי חוליות: אחת להקת
המחול הצבאית והשניה חולית הזמרים. הראשונה
ממשיכה בהופעותיה גם כיום, אך השניה נפגעה
בתאונת„דרכים בנגב וכמה מחבריה נפגעו.

חולית המחול מונה שני שחקנים, שתי רקדניות,
שני רקדנים ואקורדיוניסט אחד. הרקדנים הם יוצאי
ביה"ס לריקוד של מיה„ארבטובה ומשרתים בצבא
הסדיר.

הופעתם הראשונה היתה ב„5 בדצמבר, וההכ־
נות נמשכו כחדשיים ימים. הריקודים רובם לפי כר
ריאוגרפיה של מיה ארבטובה וקצת משל האחראי

על התוליה, ניסן יתיר, הכוונה לתת במסגרת אמבר־
חית פשוטה בידור לחיילים. הם עוסקים שעות רבות
באימונים ובהופעותיהם עד כה מוכיחות, כי המטרה
הושגה.

את הפזמונים הקליט כותב יוסף כנעני, אף הוא
איש צה"ל. התכנית המשעשעת והמבדרת נמשכת
45 דקות. התלבושות נעשו בחלקן על ידי הלהקה
עצמה וחלקן ניתנו ע"י הצבא וחיל־הים.

בין הדברים הזוכים להצלחה רבה בקרב ציבור
החיילים בולט „ריקוד האש" והקטע „פגישות של
אנשי מקצוע".

לקראת הופעת „הכסף" שלהם אני מאחלים להם
כה לחי, עלו והצליחו.

א. מרדכי

Moshiko To Teach At Dance Workshops

Moshiko, the famed Israeli choreographer, performer, and composer is coming to the JCC the weekend of September 8.

Born Moshe Itzhak-Halevy, Moshiko is the son of an old Yemenite family. For many years, he was one of the principal dancers of *Inbal*, the Yemenite dance theatre of Israel. He was also the founder/director/choreographer of *Hapa-amomim*, the Israel folk dance company which successfully toured Israel and Europe.

For the past few years Moshiko has been teaching dance in the United States. In early September, the well-known dancer will bring his classroom to the JCC. The Arts Department, in cooperation with the Dance Center of Rochester, is sponsoring two workshops and one master class.

On Saturday evening, September 8, an open workshop will be held from 8-10 p.m. A second open workshop has been scheduled for Sunday, September 9 from 2-4 p.m. The open workshop is appropriate for beginners as well as advanced students.

A master class will be held on Sunday, September 9 from 11 a.m. -

MOSHE ITZHAK-HALEVY

12:30 p.m. The master class consists of modern technique with Yemenite elements and styling.

Fees are: $3 for 1 open workshop, $5 for 2 open workshops, and $4 for the master class. If interested, you must pre-register in the Arts Office or send in the accompanying coupon. For more information, call Herb Katz, Arts Director.

MOSHIKO DANCE WORKSHOPS

Return to: JCC Arts Department, 1200 Edgewood Avenue, Rochester, N.Y. 14618

NAME_____ PHONE_____

ADDRESS_____ ZIP CODE_____

I want to register for (please check):

____ 1 Open Workshop ($3)
____ 2 Open Workshops ($5)
____ Master Class ($4)

AMOUNT ENCLOSED_____

ההסתדרות הכללית של
העובדים באריֿישראל

הועד הפועל

האגף לתרבות וחנוך

המחלקה לתרבות ולאמנות

כ"ה   באדר   תשמ"ג
10   במרס   1983

לכבוד
מושיקו יצחק-הלוי
ניר-יורק
ארה"ב

שלום רב,

תודה על מכתבך.
שוחחתי אודותיך עם תרצה הודס ועם מישראל ברזילי.
חבל לי שאתה חוזר רק בסוף שנה זו. אם היית היום בארץ
היה לנו תפקיד להציע לך, ויכולנו להפיק תועלת רבה מן
הידע והנסיון שלך בתחום המחול והפולקלור.

כשתחזור ארצה, נשמח לעשות כל מאמץ כדי לעזור לך להקלט
חזרה בתחום זה.

בברכה,

יגאל בן-נרן
יו"ר המחלקה

העתק- החֿ' תרצה הודס
מישאל ברזילי

בית הועד הפועל   רחֿ' ארלוזורוב 93 ת.ד. 303, תל-אביב
טלפון : 261111—03

יום א'
18 ביולי
ניו יורק

לידידי
מושיקו הנכבד

מאז אני טסתי חזרה לארץ
את אשר רציתי ללמוד כאן למדתי ואפילו
בהצלחה ניכרת. אני מקווה
לעשות ריקוד חדש זה באמת.
שמעתי את התקליט החדש שלך והוא
מוצלח כמו הקודמים. וגם נהניתי
מאוד מ"דודו יקראו" ומהשירה שלך. אתה
יודע שאני הוצאתי תקליט שנקרא "ארץ צבת"
ובו 13 ריקודים שלי. קנט ספיר הסכים
להפיץ את התקליט וגם לדאוג לו
כריכה ועטיפה חדשה ויפה.
למדתי בדלו סטרי׳ אצל פרד שבועיים וזה
היה מוצלח מאוד וגם בסן לואי אוניברסיטי
אבל זה לא היה כך מוצלח (מה לעשות)
השארתי לך תקליט שלי במתנה
אצל קנט ספיר וחנה בחנות שלהם
בניו-יורק. אני מקווה שתהנה ממנו
אפילו שיש בו כמה הקלטות ביתיות
שעשיתי יחד עם אשתי מתוך חוג בדירה.
ואת התקליט לא אחיד באיכותו.
בתקווה שאתה עושה חיל ומאחל לך הצלחה
רבה בדרכך. ידידך אליהו גמליאל

Ballet Ys

October 3, 1979

Moshe Itzchuk-Halevy
250 West 15th St., #H
New York City, New York
10011

Dear Moshiko:

The balance owing on your choreography fee is $500
as per the second contract. As you requested I have
made this into American Dollars and attached a money
order for the correct amount.

I have also enclosed copies of our correspondence
for your records.

The reviews of our performances have been very
good. There will be more available when the tour is
over later this month, and I will forward them to you
as they arrive.

Yours sincerely,

Gordon Pearson
General Manager

Encl.

Ballet Ys of Canada
366 Adelaide St. E.
Toronto, Canada M5A 3X9
(416) 364-3428

Greetings and Reports

בס"ד יום ד' ג בתמוז התשע"ו
13.7.2016

אלולו אלי ברק שאור ועוזר פלג ורוח
מצמה מצמה את הבריק הנכבד והנערץ
מר מושיקו האהוב והנחמד ליום הולדתו

ה' יצערך וישמריך ימציך כיום וגנשימה
ויתן לך הבלחה וגדולת לכל הימים
בבריאות אלום כוחר צור ורחיים

להאריך שנותיך בבריאות עד 120
עם חיים טובים ומאושרים לך לבעלתך
ולכל משפחתך בשמחה וגלכה ואו

שזכבת תמיך לימים טובים
בהלבה לכל האנשמה לבעם נכרים ונענ
אמן כן יהי רצון..

ונסים בברכת משירה של נעמי שמר
לו יהי לו יהי אנעו לו יהי
כל שנבקש לו יהי אמן ואמן
ותגורכו כולכם מצל עליון

מאת שלמה תרבין

לַמַר מוֹשִיקוֹ
אֲרִיכוּת יָמִים

אנושיות חדשה
ברלה

עַל אֶצַע הַגְּבָעוֹת וְהָרְכָסִים
לְאָזְנֵי דֹּר רִיזֹן,
רִיזוֹן עַל עֲתִיד הָאָדָם,
אֶרְקִי? וְזֹר, שָׁאוֹן וְשָׁעוּר.

וְרַק הוּא, פֶּן קִצֵּף,
כִּי הַבְּדִּינוֹן וְנִפְסַן צֵינוּ אִתָּם;
"מִיכָּה עַד מִשֶׁה וְכָל זֶה עַם חַיָּם",
פֵּאוֹם בַּדְּחַי, וְאוֹשִׁיעֵן פַּמֵּעַ.

וְכָן לַקְסֵם, וְ"רֵיבֵם",
רִינוֹ בֹּזֵיו אֵלֶי קְפֵמִין,
עַל "עֲם בַּרְכָס", וְלְבָּתַי אֵלֵיו,
פִּלֹר עֲלֵיזוֹ, וְזְאֵל בְּכוֹ עֲלֵיךְ.

וְשָׁוֹמֵע נְאֵלֶנוּ לָדַיִם וְזוֹן רִיב,
וְהַלַּמֵּעַ לֹא עֲלְעָה גְּמֵוּל.
וְשֶׁלֵם רִיקְדֵּים נִשְׁעֵרֵי פֹּים,
עֲלָעָם יָצִי, חַבָּה וְפִעֵין.

עַל דָּבַע נַשְׁעַךְ וְעָלֵף, פָּתוֹן וְבֵּעֵף.
וְלֹא פָּחַי אַנָּע נָדִים.
פֹּא "פֶּא אֵיֹן וְאֵל, וְאַח, רֹיו רִיו וְאֵך.
וֹזֹעֵלֵי נֹסֵךְ בְּאֵון פֵּיסַי נָבִים.

וֹרֵם זֵאן נְבֹנִי:וֹרְ, הַשֶׁאָךְ בְּצֵיזֵם אֵן מֵאוֹם.

מושיקו הלוי
האחד והיחיד
תודה והוקרה

על תרומתך רבת השנים לריקודי העם ...

אנו גאים לרקוד את ריקודייך המיוחדים

שהם נכס צאן ברזל במעגל.

תודה שבאת להתארח אצלנו בראש העין.

בהחלט גאווה לרקוד לצידך ....

לעולם אל תפסיק את עתידך בתנועה !!!!

בהערכה ואהבה
חוג ראש העין
ודודו בחזילאי

אוגוסט 2014

Danny Uziel grants me a certificate of appreciation on behalf of himself and Ruth Goodman for my contribution to Israeli folk dancing, the event took place in New York

With Danny Uziel on my 80th birthday

משה יצחק-הלוי

מלחין וכוריאוגרף יליד הארץ, שנת 1932. התפרסם בשם מושיקו יצחק הלוי.

מושיקו עוסק בעיקר בתחום ריקודי העם הישראליים, ובמהלך עבודתו נמלחין חיבר כ-150 לחנים המלווים את ריקודיו ומושמעים בארץ ובכרחבי העולם. יצירתו הראשונה הוצגה ב-1959 במסגרת פסטיבל מחולות בסכוטן שבנבליה, מיצירותיו המוכרות: "דבקה אוריה", "לו היית הנערה", "פרח זהב" רבן-יה. מושיקו הופיע בפסטיבלים באירופה וזכה במדליה בפסטיבל מחול בנבליה. ביצירתו הוא מושפע ממחזיקה אתנית תימנית, חסידית, ישראלית מודנית וערבית, וממחול מודרני, בלט קלאסי, ג'ז וסטופס. מושיקו מדריך עד היום קבוצות בסמינרים בארץ ובעולם.

Yakir Akum ceremony, 2013

From My Repertoire of Performances

Japanese singer

Hippie

Hawaiian war medley

Performing the song "Romania Romania"

"Figaro" – from the book Masibilia

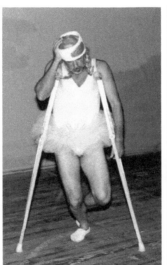

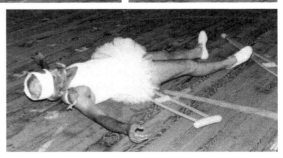

Hora Keff Mot HaBarbur talent show

A Nation's Culture is Measured by the Number of its Artists

By Moshe Yitzhak-HaLevy (Moshiko), February 2017

I first encountered this sentence at the start of my artistic journey in the field of dance, and it has accompanied me to this day, over sixty years later.

I felt the meaning and power of these words as a spoken demand and asked myself who bore the responsibility and commitment to address such a vitally important matter.

In a country with a government there are also institutions whose function is to handle various matters, including the institution of culture and art, whose role it is to take interest and discover, to support and encourage talent in all fields of art and provide sufficient financial support to allow the worthy to prioritize their art without financial concerns.

Sadly, today, more than sixty years after our state achieved independence, we still discover shameful displays of artists unable to make a dignified living and barely surviving.

The country must urgently prioritize caring for the artists who contributed, contribute and will contribute in the future as well.

Artists need peace of mind to give themselves to their work without other concerns, allowing them to maximize their talents.

The more artists multiply, the more blessed we will be and culture will thrive in our country

꧁꧂

Thank you to all the dancers in Israel and worldwide

who have accompanied me over the years, believed in me and the rightness of my path

and enjoyed my dances and melodies.

I drew encouragement, strength and inspiration from you to carry on to this very day.

> *Yours in honest friendship,*
> *Moshiko*

꧁꧂

A special thanks to the arrangers with whom I worked and who produced my compositions.

Likewise, melodies that are not mine and were rejuvenated:

1. Albert Piamente
2. Amir Froylich
3. Hertzel Bodinger
4. Chaim Hadad
5. Gabi Swissa
6. Ivy Kazaz

꧁꧂

Special thanks to Chaim Hadad z"l who arranged over sixty compositions for me,

out of love and respect for my musical contribution to society.

> *May his memory be blessed*

List of Dances from 1959 to this Day

No.	Dance Name	Video No.	Disc No.	Music	Dance Form	Year
1	Debka Uriya	3	1,11		Circle line	1959
2	Et Dodim Kalah	4	1,11		Couples	1960
3	Debka Kurdit	5	2,12	Moshiko	Circle line	1960
4	Yellow River				Line cluster	1960
5	ChaCha Mo				Line cluster	1960
6	Tefilat HaShachar	4	1,11		Circle	1961
7	HaHelech	3	1,11		Circle line	1965
8	Kissufim		2,12		Couples circle	1966
9	Ki Hivshilu Eshkolot	1	1,11		Circle	1968
10	Dror Yikra		3,4 2,12		Couples	1970
11	Ga'aguim	1	2,12	Moshiko	Circle	1971
12	Etkashet li Beabaya	4	1,11		Circle	1973
13	Debka Bedouit		1,11		Circle line	1973
14	HaMecholelet	5	1,11		Couples	1973
15	Lemaana		1,11		Couples	1973
16	En Adir		2,12		Couples	1973
17	Hora Chemed		2,12	Moshiko	Circle	1973
18	Mechol HaDvash	4	2,12		Circle line	1973
19	Mishal	5	2,12		Circle line	1973

No.	Dance Name	Video No.	Disc No.	Music	Dance Form	Year
20	Se'e Yona	2	2*3,4		Circle	1974
21	Eshal Elohai		3,4		Circle	1975
22	BeTof Utzlil	4	3,4	Moshiko	Circle	1975
23	Hamavdil		3,4		Circle	1975
24	Ya Abud		3,4		Circle line	1975
25	Marhaba		3,4	Moshiko	Circle line	1975
26	Al Yadil	2	3,4		Circle line	1975
27	Tinten Banat		3,4		Couples	1975
28	Tamah Temima	5	3,4		Couples	1975
29	Da'ase		3,4		Circle line	1976
30	Hey Yo Ya		3,4	Moshiko	Circle line	1976
31	Ya Habib	5	3,4		Circle	1976
32	Yossel Yossel	5	3,4		Line cluster	1976
33	Yelelat HaRuach	5	3,4	Moshiko	Couples	1976
34	Yesh Li Gan		3,4		Circle	1976
35	Machol HaShnayim		3,4	Moshiko	Couples	1976
36	Oneg Shabbat		3,4		Circle	1976
37	Smadar		2,12		Circle	1977
38	Zakariya		3,4	Moshiko	Circle line	1977
39	Shema Yisrael		5,6	Moshiko	Circle	1977
40	El HaAyin				Circle	1977
41	Hora Yamit		5,6	Moshiko	Circle	1978

No.	Dance Name	Video No.	Disc No.	Music	Dance Form	Year
42	HaMangina Sheli	4	5,6	Moshiko	Couples	1978
43	Zafeh		5,6	Moshiko	Couples	1978
44	Yaffo		5,6	Moshiko	Circle line	1978
45	Neima Tajikit		5,6		Couples	1978
46	Uri Tzafon		5,6		Circle	1978
47	Alei Givah		5,6		Couples	1978
48	Chiribim		5,6		Couples	1978
49	Shema HaEl		5,6		Circle	1978
50	HaReshut		1,11		Couples	1980
51	Avi Avi		5,6	Moshiko	Circle line	1980
52	Bosmat		5,6	Moshiko	Circle	1980
53	HaEmek Hu Chalom		5,6		Circle	1980
54	Har HaTzofim		5,6		Circle	1980
55	UveYom HaShabbat		5,6	Moshiko	Circle	1980
56	VeHashem MiTzion Yishag		5,6	Moshiko	Circle	1980
57	Yam Hatchelet		5,6	Moshiko	Couples	1980
58	Lo Sharti Lach Artzi		5,6		Circle	1980
59	Lefelach HaRimon		5,6		Circle	1980
60	Tel Giborim	2	5,6	Moshiko	Circle line	1980
61	BaMishol		7,8		Couples	1983
62	Mechol HaMezeg	1	7,8		Circle	1983
63	Masoret		7,8		Circle	1983

No.	Dance Name	Video No.	Disc No.	Music	Dance Form	Year
64	Kirya Yefeifia	2	7,8		Circle	1983
65	Sachki Sachki	5	7,8		Circle	1983
66	Zer Shirim	4	3,4	Moshiko	Couples	1984
67	Kinneret	1	7,8		Circle	1984
68	Renanim		7,8	Moshiko	Couples	1984
69	Shababe		7,8	Moshiko	Circle line	1984
70	Shevach Lael		7,8		Couples	1984
71	Vesamachta Bechageicha	1	3,4	Moshiko	Couples	1985
72	Bashvilim		7,8	Moshiko	Circle	1985
73	Hadouni		7,8		Circle line	1985
74	Hitahavti BaZemer	4	7,8		Couples	1985
75	Mor		7,8	Moshiko	Circle	1985
76	Mizmor LeDavid		7,8	Moshiko	Circle	1985
77	Mi Kamocha	5	7,8	Moshiko	Couples	1985
78	Reich Hadas	5	7,8	Moshiko	Couples	1985
79	Debka K'naan		2,12		Circle line	1986
80	Shir LaEmek	4	5,6		Circle	1986
81	Debka Dor		7,8	Moshiko	Circle line	1986
82	Dilam Bazan	5	7,8	Moshiko	Couples	1986
83	Veshavu Banim	3	7,8	Moshiko	Circle	1986
84	Al Levavi	5	7,8	Moshiko	Couples	1987
85	BeLev HaLeyl		7,8		Circle	1988

No.	Dance Name	Video No.	Disc No.	Music	Dance Form	Year
86	Perach Zahav	1	7,8	Moshiko	Circle	1988
87	Ariel		9,10	Moshiko	Circle line	1988
88	Jettili		9,10		Circle line	1988
89	Yam Tichon	3	9,10	Moshiko	Circle	1988
90	Ma Tov		9,10	Moshiko	Couples	1988
91	Noffim	2	9,10	Moshiko	Circle	1988
92	Odeh Yah	1	9,10	Moshiko	Circle	1989
93	Ben-Yah		9,10	Moshiko	Circle line	1989
94	Galei HaMizrach	5	9,10	Moshiko	Circle	1989
95	Lach	1	9,10	Moshiko	Circle	1989
96	Netafim	3	9,10	Moshiko	Couples	1989
97	Tzeada	3	9,10	Moshiko	Circle line	1989
98	Elef Laila		9,10	Moshiko	Circle	1990
99	Bracha		9,10	Moshiko	Circle	1990
100	Debka Adi		9,10	Moshiko	Circle line	1990
101	Hora Esh		9,10	Moshiko	Circle	1990
102	Chalomot		9,10	Moshiko	Circle	1990
103	Yiska		9,10	Moshiko	Circle	1990
104	Kochav HaRuach		9,10	Moshiko	Circle	1990
105	Ayuma		9,10	Moshiko	Circle	1991
106	As'al	1	9,10	Moshiko	Couples	1991
107	Libbi	5	9,10	Moshiko	Couples	1991
108	Mechol Gruzini	1	9,10	Moshiko	Circle line	1991

No.	Dance Name	Video No.	Disc No.	Music	Dance Form	Year
109	Nishmat Kol Hai		9,10	Moshiko	Circle	1991
110	Vals HaShoshanim	1	1,11	Moshiko	Couples	1993
111	Yakir Menachem	1	1,11	Moshiko	Circle	1993
112	Alizut	1	1,11	Moshiko	Circle	1993
113	Shatiach Parsi	1	1,11	Moshiko	Circle	1993
114	Shovevut	2	1,11	Moshiko	Couples	1993
115	Shirat HaYam	1	1,11	Moshiko	Circle	1993
116	Ashira LaShem			Moshiko	Circle	1993
117	BeLev Sameach	2	1,11	Moshiko	Circle	1994
118	Vals LaTikva	2	1,11	Moshiko	Circle	1994
119	BaAyara	2	2,12	Moshiko	Circle	1994
120	Beklilut	3	2,12	Moshiko	Circle	1994
121	Dalit	3	2,12	Moshiko	Circle	1994
122	Lu Hayit HaNa'ara	2	2,12	Moshiko	Circle line	1994
123	Mizrach Maarav	3	2,12	Moshiko	Circle line	1994
124	Nina	3	2,12	Moshiko	Circle	1994
125	Saharane	3	2,12	Moshiko	Circle line	1994
126	Ura Yisrael	3	2,12	Moshiko	Circle	1994
127	Vals HaNigun		14	Moshiko	Couples	1995
128	Gam Li El		14	Moshiko	Circle	1996
129	Hora Li		14	Moshiko	Circle	1996
130	Vals LaOhavim		14	Moshiko	Couples	1996
131	Cholot Lohatim		14	Moshiko	Circle line	1996

No.	Dance Name	Video No.	Disc No.	Music	Dance Form	Year
132	Omer		14	Moshiko	Circle	1996
133	Alumim		14	Moshiko	Circle	1997
134	Bouki Dalale				Circle	1997
135	HaGeula		14	Moshiko	Circle	1998
136	Et Ashir		14	Moshiko	Circle line	1998
137	Reichan		14	Moshiko	Circle	1998
138	Eretz Ahuva		15	Moshiko	Circle line	1998
139	Etgar		15	Moshiko	Circle	1998
140	Yanuka		15	Moshiko	Circle	1998
141	Yisrapiko		15	Moshiko	Couples	1998
142	Abda bak				Couples	1998
143	Ana Lak	4			Couples	1998
144	Haidel Haidel				Circle	1998
145	Halevai Alai	4			Circle	1998
146	Yumati				Circle	1998
147	Ke'ev Rosh	4			Circle	1998
148	San'a	4			Circle	1998
149	Shemesh Yaffa			Moshiko	Circle	1998
150	Sara'le	4			Circle	1998
151	HaShofar		15	Moshiko	Circle	1999
152	Sodot Midbar		15	Moshiko	Circle	1999
153	E-Lai		15	Moshiko	Circle	1999
154	Cherkes		15	Moshiko	Circle line	1999

No.	Dance Name	Video No.	Disc No.	Music	Dance Form	Year
155	Tzur Eli		15	Moshiko	Circle	1999
156	Tzame				Circle line	2000
157	Ashuri		15	Moshiko	Circle line	2001
158	Eshet Chail		15	Moshiko	Couples	2001
159	Gamla		15	Moshiko	Circle line	2001
160	Dma'ot Ahava		15	Moshiko	Circle	2001
161	Hodu LaShem		15	Moshiko	Circle	2001
162	Diwan		15	Moshiko	Circle	2002
163	Kol Od		15	Moshiko	Circle	2002
164	HeChalil		15		Circle	2003
165	Shabbat Malkah		15	Moshiko	Circle	2003
166	Al Lanu			Moshiko	Circle	2003
167	Yimloch HaShem			Moshiko	Circle	2003
168	Yishkeni			Moshiko	Couples	2003
169	Mavani				Lines in front of the music	2003
170	Odeni Yalda			Moshiko	Circle line	2003
171	Atari			Moshiko	Circle	2003
172	Rava Dolta				Lines	2003
173	Pa'am Hayinu		16	Moshiko	Couples	2005
174	Shir Preda		16	Moshiko	Circle	2005
175	Sirta-Mosh		16	Moshiko	Lines - Circle	2005

No.	Dance Name	Video No.	Disc No.	Music	Dance Form	Year
176	Shuvi HaShulamit		16	Moshiko	Circle	2005
177	Bereshit		16		Circle	2005
178	Moshi-Tanas		16	Moshiko	Circle	2005
179	Pgisha Mikrit		16	Moshiko	Couples	2005
180	Fussai-ko		16	Moshiko	Circle	2005
181	Ya Halali Ya Mali		16		Circle	2005
182	Mizmor Shir		16	Moshiko	Circle	2005
183	Targil Teimani		16	Moshiko	Circle	2005
184	E-Mi yoladeti		16	Moshiko	Circle	2005
185	Lo Eten		16	Moshiko	Circle	2005
186	Amok Balev		16	Moshiko	Lines	2005
187	Betzet Chatan		16	Moshiko	Circle	2005
188	Talaa		16		Lines	2005
189	Yuvali		17	Moshiko	Circle	2007
190	Avnei HaHoshen		17	Moshiko	Circle	2007
191	Ani Zocher		17	Moshiko	Circle	2007
192	At Kmo Shir		17	Moshiko	Circle	2007
193	Balkan		17	Moshiko	Circle line	2007
194	Shai L'Eilah		17	Moshiko	Circle	2007
195	Nijad		17	Moshiko	Circle line	2007
196	Kurdinash		17	Moshiko	Circle line	2007
197	Yom Ezkerah		17	Moshiko	Circle	2007
198	Nerot Shabbat		17	Moshiko	Circle	2007

No.	Dance Name	Video No.	Disc No.	Music	Dance Form	Year
199	Vals LaMiya-Ar		17	Moshiko	Circle	2007
200	Tefilat HaDerech		17	Moshiko	Circle	2007
201	Haleluya		17	Moshiko	Rondo	2007
202	Ulu		18		Lines	2009
203	Hallo		18		Lines	2009
204	Sherine		18		Circle	2009
205	Moti		18	Moshiko	Circle	2009
206	Shir L'Ofir		18	Moshiko	Circle	2009
207	Leshachaf		18	Moshiko	Circle	2009
208	BeKetzev Teimani		18	Moshiko	Circle	2009
209	HaShabbat Hi Lanu		18	Moshiko	Circle	2009
210	Vals Avivi		18	Moshiko	Circle	2009
211	Chamisha Revaim		18	Moshiko	Circle	2009
212	Hayiti Rotze		18	Moshiko	Circle	2009
213	Debka Gabis		18	Gabi Souisa	Circle	2009
214	Nolad Lanu Neched			Moshiko	Lines	2011
215	Ya Bouy				Circle line	2012
216	Ya Salaam				Circle	2012
217	Edi			Moshiko	Lines	2012
218	Tamar HaKtana			Moshiko	Circle	2013
219	Ana - Ani				Circle	2014
220	Suddenly You Love Me				Couples	2014

No.	Dance Name	Video No.	Disc No.	Music	Dance Form	Year
221	Dublin				Lines	2014
222	Tarakan				Circle line	2014
223	Bombay				Lines	2014
224	Yaffa At Rayati			Moshiko	Couples	2014
225	Yalda Yaffa				Circle	2015
226	Sirtaki				Lines	2015
227	Masri				Lines	2015
228	El Adon				Circle	2015
229	Zichronot MiKurdistan				Circle	2015
230	Az Barnadam				Circle line	2015
231	El Adon Ashkenazi				Circle	2015
232	Tunisai				Circle	2016
233	Neimat HaShouk				Circle	2016
234	Eshet Chayil Avi Ben Israel				Circle	2016
235	Neima Targil Boker				Lines	2016
236	Hanichi Li				Circle	2016
237	Ti-Rash-Rash				Circle	2016
238	Mazurka Li			Moshiko	Couples	2016
239	Yesh Li Perach BeGani			Moshiko	TBD	2016
240	Vals LeOri			Moshiko	Circle	2017

Lightning Source UK Ltd.
Milton Keynes UK
UKHW051003080321
379970UK00002B/18